Escaping The Pen:
How Lessons from Doing Time Can Set You Free

Written by:
King B
And
Buddy Love

Cadmus Publishing
www.cadmuspublishing.com

DEDICATION:

First off, we dedicate this book to our incredible mothers who not only verbally gave us words that cultivated mindsets of true freedom, but showed us through their life that no matter what condition nor circumstances we may find ourselves, we are never defeated as long as we are 'free in our minds.' To Franzetta K. Haddick and Vishandis Walker. This book is also for all those who find themselves 'confined,' mentally, emotionally, physically, and spiritually throughout the world.

FOREWORD

There's a universal proverb that says, "It takes a nation to raise a child." While this proverb rings true, in direct juxtaposition there's a very troubling dilemma manifesting in the collective conscience of society, avalanching through the lives of millions of families. We seem to forget that the transcendent fact of time and space is no respecter of persons. Time and space march forward; the past flows into the moment as the future swallows the now. All the while creating new beginnings and endings. It is this reality that looms large in the lives of families the world over. If it takes a nation to raise a child, what would it take to raise a child of a man? From the smallest 'white lie' to the most horrendous crime against humanity, all can be traced back to a childhood occurrence that morphed into a dysfunctional 'stronghold.' Intimacy in the hand of a child becomes unchecked sexual immorality. Poverty ushers in rank competitivities, drowning morality in its wake. The will to power becomes a bludgeoning tool when there's a baby at the wheel.

Penal institutions hold the most concentrated populaces of this caliber of man. Society may view this phenomenon as an egregious dilemma and on the surface, one must admit that, but what we as a society seem to forget is the duality of what has happened versus what is happening. There are only three institution that create the novelty of leisure time. Military, academia, and penal institutions are the common thread of this fabric. Military provides one's bare necessities so that the focus of the human soul and its physical resources are in accord with the designed agenda and mission. Academic institutions provide housing, food, and etcetera through financial aid for the same reasons illustrated above. Penal institutions provide prisoners with time and necessitates as 'wards' of the state for the sole purpose of punishment and prevention. Within the framework of doing time there's a saying amongst prisoners: "Are you doing time or are you letting time do you?" How one answers the question on a daily basis will make the difference between capitalization through creativity or codependency leading to reincarceration.

Christ told Nicodemus, "Unless you so be reborn you cannot see the kingdom of heaven." Unless the little boy/girl is healed by the amniotic fluids of reflection, contemplation, and rumination, recidivism will rule the day in the lives of hundreds of thousands of prisoners. This is the water that Christ offers for the drought terrain of the soul. There are three types of prisoners doing time who are shaped through the internalization of the daily drip of incarceration. The first category type continues the vain mission of a rebel without a cause—he thumbs his nose at authority and rules at every opportunity possible. With each provocation and disciplinary infraction, he's constrained in the tighter vice of immobility. He doesn't seem to realize that there rests, in his darkened heart, the enemy of his soul. What started as a slow drip has become an acidic flow of isolation. Like magma flows of hot lava over the flesh, all senses have been singed in the fiery perdition of administrative segregation. Each sensory experience seems to become one gigantic moment in time. His actions and attitudes have so captured his circumstances that 23 hours a day he's left to ponder the very thing that he's always feared—Self.

The second category type is the prisoner who fully embraces his experience of doing time. Actually, he lays on the altar of sacrifice fully surrendering all of self. After years of incarceration, he becomes 'Mr. Penitentiary,' every fabric and nuance of his soul reeks of incarceration. He has become a new creation in the Stockholm Syndrome effect. He becomes so immersed in the things of prison that he has literally disqualified himself from the future things of society. The prison house has become his prison home. He has convinced himself that there is uncertainty in society but certainty in prison. Predictability is his best friend and if nothing else, prison is predictable. He has allowed himself to be drowned in the 'cumulative waters of time.'

There is a third category of prisoners who understand that time is precious. They will willfully and intentionally begin to rummage through the wreckage of a destructive heart to salvage the submerged essence of who they are. They understand that asking and answering three fundamental questions are essential to develop lifestyle: Who am I? What is my purpose? What is my destiny? The prison experience is forged into a prison experiment. Leisure time is used as a fabricating tool to shape, fashion, and mold the environment into a breeding ground for success. Ideas are formulated as experiential knowledge. This knowledge builds concepts that lay in the foundational tenants of morals, principles, and values. What seems to be an insurmountable task in such a chaotic environment actually morphs into what I will term "power perspective." Power is the ability to describe a phenomenon and make it act in a desired manner. Through the methodology of checks and balances, one's values become consistently an extension of one's views.

This category of man has taken his sword of destruction and his piercing spear of rebellion and beat it into tools of change to not only transform self, but the society that he once wreaked havoc in.

Ryan Moody
Cofield Unit/2020

CONTENTS

INTRODUCTION

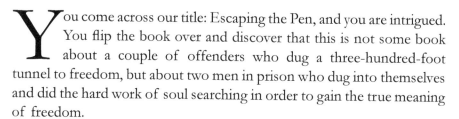

You come across our title: Escaping the Pen, and you are intrigued. You flip the book over and discover that this is not some book about a couple of offenders who dug a three-hundred-foot tunnel to freedom, but about two men in prison who dug into themselves and did the hard work of soul searching in order to gain the true meaning of freedom.

Then you scratch your head and a small question enters your mind- why should I listen to someone in prison? I am out here in society as a productive member. What can someone in prison teach me? Well, I'm glad you asked.

First, I would like to point out something that a lot of people simply fail to take into account--part of one of the most prolific books of all time was written in a prison. It's one of the top-selling books of all time and has inspired some of the greatest transformations the world has ever seen. Maybe you've already guessed it, The Holy Bible.

Paul, while in the solitude of his cell, wrote a big portion of the New Testament. He could have easily written these pages in the free society where a wealth of materials was at his disposal, or even the best of scribes who would have offered their services to such a great man. Ralph Walden Emerson once said, 'When it is dark enough, you can see the stars." We can imagine Paul in his darkest moment finally finding the words within his Soul that were meant for the world, connecting with his purpose and deciding to share it with the world. We don't have to imagine because the book that you are now reading was forged in the same type of darkness and we now share our souls with the world.

Another great leader who rose from the grime of the street and entered the prison system also left a lasting legacy after his incarceration: Malcom X (1925-1965). He was known as 'Detroit Red' in the streets. He entered the prison system just as many other young black men before him, stuck in the cycle of the system. With a lack of distraction bombarding his mind and heart, looking for something different, Malcom began a journey in prison that would impact an entire culture and influence many great young leaders for generations to come. It seems as if in the streets, Malcom was incarcerated mentally in a cycle of destruction that kept him enslaved. But, through the darkness and solitude of prison, he was able to connect with what he was destined for. We understand the solitude and darkness of prison can be turned into a tool that liberates the soul and sets your life on a course of true destiny. We understand because this is our journey and just as a farmer takes dung and turns it into a tool of growth, we have learned this secret and, in this book, we share it with you for your life.

The last two historical figures we used as examples we never got to meet, even though their life has touched ours. Our brother and close friend, Ryan Moody, who graciously wrote the forward, is a living witness to what it means to 'escape the pen.' We will get deeper into the particular details of his story later in the book, but when you enter Moody's presence you can feel his spiritual, mental, and emotional power. Despite his potential incarceration for life, he has mastered the art of being free internally. He is a living witness of how prison can be used as a tool of true liberation and how those lessons can be passed on to others. Everywhere he goes he takes his freedom with him and does his best to live this truth. We know the principles that we are about to share can change your life and set you free because our minds and hearts have been transformed; we are just saving you a prison trip. You're welcome. :)

If handing you lessons that we had to gain through hard time isn't enough motivation for you, we would like to add that combined, we have over twenty years of 'doing' time and not just 'passing' it.

On a daily basis, it is not hard to encounter a man or woman in society or prison who, when you ask 'what's up?' responds, "just maintaining," "just tryna make it," or "passing time, bro." Most of these individuals, if you had a chance to watch them for a day, you would see them just going through the motions without passion or direction. See, to us, 'passing time' is passive. A common definition of passive is, "accepting what happens without resisting or trying to change anything." People like this are slaves to the system and blindly follow the path that is laid out for them to follow. We see it here in prison everyday where TV, games, drugs, and 'penitentiary games,' are used as devices to distract individuals from taking responsibility for the outcomes of their lives.

'Doing' is a verb. It requires action. A person doing their time is actively executing the vision they have set forth for themselves and not just following or accepting what comes. So, when we say that we have been doing time, we are essentially saying that you can trust that we have been doing our time, we are essentially saying that you can trust the principles that we are about share because what you now hold in your hands is evidence that though our bodies are locked up, our minds have found the true keys to liberation. We have used our incarceration as a tool to find our way out of the internal limits that have held us back for so long.

Not only is the book that you are now reading evidence of our mentality of 'doing' our time, but between the both of us, we have college degrees and over twenty plus years of life skills, courses, and trades that we have capitalized on here in prison.

Combined, we have read well over five hundred fiction and non-fiction titles such as Think and Grow Rich, Mastery, The Road Less Travelled, etc.

We are both very passionate about fitness and have transformed our bodies by adding an average of twenty pounds of muscle to the frames that we came into prison with. We are workout partners and we push each other daily to be diligent about today and not using yesterday as an excuse to slack.

Spiritually we are both still growing and evolving and we have a healthy appreciation for the Creator who gave us this world filled with possibilities.

Each day we plant seeds mentally, physically, and spiritually. In a days' time, if an individual would 'do' something that contributed to his mental sharpness and growth, if he would stimulate his body in a way that reduced stress and improved overall health, and walk in constant appreciation spiritually-aware and connected to his creator; this individual would know the difference between just being alive and actually living.

Yes, we know these truths, but the sad reality is that a countless number of people are trapped and stuck behind mental and emotional walls and can't find the keys of release. James Allen said it this way: "People are anxious to improve their circumstances but are unwilling to improve themselves, they are therefore bound." My coauthor, Buddy, says it this way: "No one can give you freedom; freedom comes when you open your mind."

We find people from all walks of life, different cultures, and socioeconomic backgrounds blame their environments, relationships, and jobs for the 'caged' conditions that control the direction and energy of their lives. The truth is that it's never our circumstances that enslaves us. Dr. M. Scott Peck, M.D. said that a lot of people use external things and people to "escape from freedom," in essence to give responsibility over to something outside ourselves. Dr. Peck said, "The difficulty we have in accepting responsibility for our behavior lies in the desire to avoid the pain of the consequences of that behavior."

What has so many people internally incarcerated is not the condition of their lives, but the condition of their minds. Throughout this book we will share with you how, despite being locked in a physical prison, we escaped into ourselves and now have a strong desire to share our freedom with you in hope that your cages will also open within. It's our desire to show you the keys that already lie waiting inside you that confine you. In the end, it's our hope that you will know and understand and then apply through wisdom, the truth that no circumstance can enslave you when your mind is free.

You are about to go on a fifteen-year journey of growth with us. During this journey of enlightenment, we will highlight unique aspects of prison life we used as tools to set our minds free and transform our lives.

We will touch on unique aspects from prison such as the intake/line class system and how it is related to the systems we start off in out in society that can seem to confine us to the perceived limitations of those starting points in life.

We will highlight the cell and how it is designed as a place of confinement and restraint, a place that is dark and meant to keep you from the light. This place can actually be used as a place of growth and development, a place for soul-searching to find the keys to your freedom. In the "Keys to Freedom" at the end of each chapter, Buddy will write and give you keys from his perspective that cap off the chapter.

You have just been sentenced to "do" fifteen years, my friend. We see potential in you and have decided to take you under our wing and "lace you up" on the ins and outs of prison life and how to maximize and "do" your time, not allowing it to do you. "Let's Ride!"

YEAR #1 INTAKE

The where and how we start off in this life is out of your hands. We can't choose our parents, their education level, how much money they have, what neighborhoods they live in, or their temperament. It is said that over half of who we are and what we become comes from the home where we grew up and the neighborhoods where we roamed. Around about the age of fifteen or sixteen, the direction of our lives starts to be largely in our hands and our decisions start to chart a course based on the vision that we hold in our minds. For my co-author and I, those decisions took a turn and one turn led us to another starting point—the intake process.

The intake process is designed to make you feel stripped of your identity and out of control. As you enter this process, everything you knew is gone. You're wide-eyed, don't know what to expect, and you're trying to process a million bits of information at once. You are herded into a large processing area where you are told to "strip out." Everyone is looking at one another, not really knowing what to do or who will go first. One by one, you are stripped naked and told to bend over and spread your cheeks. The humiliation some experience at this moment leads to a lost of self-respect and they never regain a sense of self from this point forward.

Next, you are told to sit in a barber chair, and you are stripped of your individualism as your head is shaved bald. You are then crowded into a shower with twenty or thirty other men for a three-minute shower. Three minutes means three minutes, a lot of men are surprised when the water cuts off and they are left with a body full of soap.

From this point on, everything is recorded and will be used to determine where you start. The photograph and identification department will take your fingerprints and enter you into a database that will be able to flag you for future crimes that link to your prints. Your picture is taken and that will be used to make you an I.D., and any identifying scars or tats are examined and recorded. Most of this information is sent to the FBI for future profiling.

Everything is moving so fast; you are being analyzed from every angle and you feel exposed. You are given a physical examination by the medical department to determine any special or chronic medical issues. A mental health screening is given to determine if medication or counseling will be needed during the duration of your sentence. In order to numb their new realities, some individuals play the 'psych card' and end up walking zombies for the duration of passing their time.

Within a few days you will receive a 'lay-in,' a pass directing you to a particular place, to go and watch an orientation video that will give you a basic breakdown on everything from PREA (Prison Rape Elimination Act), the general rules, how to file a grievance, programs that are provided such as substance abuse, and the parole process.

In the next interview, information is gathered to determine your thinking patterns and how you tend to express those thoughts. Classification will use this information to determine where you start in the prison system concerning the unit you will spend most of your time at, what job you will start out doing, what general area you will be housed in, and your overall security needs.

In this interview, every decision that has led you to prison will be analyzed. You will be asked about your criminal history based off any police files obtained from the county you came from; you will be asked about your social history to determine any gang affiliations. Your educational history/IQ will be assessed to determine your mental capabilities. You will be asked about your father and mother's histories so that they can determine any generational habits that have been passed down. They inform you that if you lie about anything during this process, you can and will be given a disciplinary case and punished.

State Classification (SCC) and Central Records Office (CRO) are sent all this information and any other pertinent information to determine really just one thing—where you start.

In society we find these same tactics of gathering information on us in order to determine where we start or where we belong. Potential employers ask for a resume to determine what skills you have and, if hired, where you will start in the company.

Educational institutions ask for a transcript in order to see if you fit in their school, and if you do, what your starting point will be and what will be required of you in order for you to be successful. If you think about it, even in our personal lives, say when we go on a date with someone we just met, we are asked questions like what are your values, when was your last serious relationship, where do you work, and what are your dreams.

These and other questions are asked in order to determine who you are and what will be the starting point of the connection—a one-night stand or a potential partner.

Everywhere we turn it is as if we are being analyzed in order to be placed where we belong, where we will start at. And most likely, our starting points are determined by the decisions and choices that we made before we got to that point. Just like in prison, we don't get to decide if the unit we are assigned to is close or far from our hometown, or what job we are given, or the block we are assigned to live on. These are mostly determined by our past actions.

Some of the choices that we make limit us for life in certain ways, but over time, we see that a starting point can be changed and overcome.

In prison you are given a custody level that limits where you can work and live. For example, if you are convicted of a sex crime, you most likely will never work in jobs like commissary or classification where "free world" women and men work. Sex crimes even keep you from attending special events that are held on the unit like Day with Dad, an event where dads spend the day playing games with their kids. You could be a model prisoner for thirty years and still never be afforded these opportunities. A man in prison can get his Master's and get out in society and stay out of trouble for the rest of his life, and never be able to become a professional doctor because he has a felony. Yes, some choices will limit us in some areas for the rest of our life, but those things don't mean you are stuck, defeated, or have to be discouraged.

Take, for example, that in prison a G3 custody level is the starting point for an individual with over fifty years. This individual (throughout the book we are doing our best not to use the words 'inmate' or 'offender.' We are men and women in prison) must live in a specific general area for ten years before he/she can live and work in certain places.

I remember walking down the run (hallway) one day and I notice this black/Hispanic-looking dude with tats all over his face. Most dudes who go that far in the tat game know that they will never taste the free air again and this is a way for them to take back a part of the individuality that was taken from them.

In the old days, the chow hall (cafeteria) was a place where after you got your tray of food, you went and sat with your people. These days, when you get your tray, they fill the tables in the order that we come off the line. So, if yo' homie ain't right behind you, he most likely will be sitting at another table. This is how I ended up being at the table with ol' boy with the tats all over his face.

I nodded my head towards him, "What's up bro?" He nodded back and said, "Coolin'," and took a bite to eat because you might get eight minutes to finish on a good day.

I said, "I see you on Z wing bro, I couldn't imagine being stuck on one wing for ten years around the same people and nobody really got nothing to lose. I don't see how you do it, bro."

He looked up between bites and smiled, "It ain't easy, but awhile back something stood out to me about the end of the serenity prayer. The prayer says, 'grant me the serenity to accept the things I cannot change, the courage to change the things I can, *and the wisdom to know the difference.*' See bro, a lot of people stress over things that's out they control and waste a lot of emotional energy that could be used in other areas. Me, I focus on my thinking and my vision. I leave the rest to God."

All I could do was nod my head as I put another spoonful of food in my mouth. The officer came and knocked on our table and said it was time for us to go. I shook his hand and found out he called himself Six.

This was one of my first encounters of seeing true freedom. I left that encounter feeling inspired and starting to understand that it's not about where you start in life, but where you see yourself finishing (vision). I started to understand that our thinking played a huge part in the way our lives turned out and that we aren't slaves to our circumstances but to our enslaving thoughts.

His attitude towards life reminded me of a quote I once ready by Wayne Dyer, "You're not stuck where you are unless [you] decide to be." That encounter taught me that being stuck was a choice, a mindset of hopelessness, a learned helplessness.

Researcher Martin Seligman saw this learned helplessness in an experiment with dogs he had strapped to a harness. The dogs received repeated shocks over and over again with no way of escaping. When the dogs were put in a situation where 'they could escape', instead of running off they just cowered in fear. They had learned helplessness.

I've seen this condition in people, also. After repeated loss, painful events, and trauma, we sometimes become stuck in a mental state of despair. But, Six taught me that this condition is a choice and that it's not where you start out in life, but where you finish.

Three years later I ended up on a general population dorm with Six and we shook hands. He had served his time on Z-wing and was now working in the kitchen as a cook by focusing on the things that he could control and allowing the results to handle themselves, he was able to use the energy that he would have wasted stressing on things that were not in his power. It was a powerful lesson for me.

The helpless state that we are speaking about was a true reality for Buddy early in life. Growing up, he struggled in school. He would be so frustrated at times from the work he was assigned that he would get migraine headaches. The struggle just got too real and so he decided to drop out at the age of seventeen. With no real education under his belt, his job opportunities were far, few, and in between. He felt stagnated, stuck, working in dead-end jobs that had him feeling empty. These and other emotions lead him to a 'starting point' of selling drugs. The decisions that he had to make in order to maintain this lifestyle are the decisions that lead him to the white heat of prison life.

I once came across a quote written by Mildred Witte Stouven, "A clay pot sitting in the sun will always be a clay pot, it has to go through the white heat of the furnace to become porcelain."

His starting point on the journey of enlightenment started with his choice to drop out of school, this choice led him to the white heat that transformed him. One of the things that he realized in the end was that there are no shortcuts to true greatness! One must see his/her dream and then grind daily in the acquisition of the dream. Instead of grinding harder on his work in school for understanding, he felt helpless and tried to take a shortcut. He took the common road and not the one less traveled.

Through Buddy's story we can see that most of our starting points in life stem from decisions that we make in attempt to escape the heat of the furnace, the struggles of life. Buddy was attempting to escape the mental and emotional frustration that came with understanding his schoolwork, but in reality, it's inside the frustration and confusion that we grow most. Teachers intentionally give us problems to solve knowing that through the process of solving them we will make the mental connections that will lead to growth. When we choose to copy off our classmate's paper, or cheat in some form (take shortcuts), we miss out on the natural overcoming spirit that clicks on inside of us as humans and goes to work to solve problems.

When you cut yourself, the body instantly knows what is needed to fix and heal the wound. You don't have to tell your blood cells to go to work, in discomfort they do what they do naturally. If Buddy would have kept at his studies, his mind would have naturally picked up on his mental frustration and went to work to understand and overcome his frustration. When we take shortcuts in order to avoid pain and frustration we miss out on the miraculous transformational power of discomfort. It is in prison that a lot of men/women use this same discomfort to transform their lives. Those who try to avoid this discomfort through penitentiary games end up worse. Coming in fresh into the prison system, one feels lost and powerless. Everything has been stripped from you. You feel naked and exposed and they want to remind you of this at every turn. At the Middleton Intake Unit in Abilene, Texas, the showers are situated at the front of the dayroom, the room where you gather to watch TV and play games. Right behind the TVs sit the showers, so as you take a shower you are on display to anyone who wants to look. It's a constant reminder of your new reality and they want you to feel powerless and out of control.

Those who survive this intake process understand that true power and control is not in the intake/classification system, just as in society, the power is not in the neighborhoods or circumstances that we sometimes have to start in. True power is in perspective! A common definition for perspective is "a way of seeing something."

Going through the intake system, Buddy and I both chose to see what they were trying to do—break and redefine us as humans.

Instead of avoiding the pain and discomfort of our situation, we embraced the struggle and used it as motivation We turned it into white heat. Those who lose themselves at certain starting points give over their power to the circumstance and they embrace the condition as their reality. In an attempt to avoid the discomfort of the situation, they do their best to become one with it. Those who become one are those who join gangs and cliques in an attempt to regain some form of their stripped identity. Those who feel exposed and naked and can't bear it any longer, cover up with homosexuality as a form of comfort. It is as if they feel they are taking control of their exposure.

Those of us who have to start our life off in the 'hood choose to eat rather than be eaten. We embrace the lifestyles that surround us daily and we smoke weed and party as a distraction to escape the reality of the struggle that we face every day. We become one with the hood mentality. This new identity, this illusion, becomes us as clay pots sitting in the sun hoping and wishing that somehow, we will turn into porcelain. It never happens though, and so, it takes more weed, more parties, and more illusions to cover the pain. We either end up dead in the streets or we end up getting sent to prison, like Buddy and I, where the real work can begin. I'm reminded of a story I once read called *Calum's Road*. Malcolm "Calum" MacLeod had spent most of his life on the Scottish island of Raasay. Calum was frustrated and felt anguished over his local governments refusal to build a road that would allow people to come and visit his property. The road limitation was so bad that the population in the area had dwindled down to just two people: Calum and his wife.

Calum was in his fifties when in 1964 he grabbed an axe, a shovel, a chopper, a wheelbarrow, and other tools, and went to work on building his own road. 10 years later, Calum finished the 1.75-mile road with grit and determination. The government even came behind him and paved the road. Calum is a true example of transforming frustration into motivation. When we don't avoid discomfort but embrace it, use it, something happens in us that naturally goes to work to fix it. We grow from the white heat.

A lot of us start out this life as clay pots in the sun, allowing our circumstances to dictate how we feel about ourselves and rob us of our hope and potential of where we can go and what we can become.

But, just as prison served as the white heat that transformed our minds into porcelain, don't allow where you are right now mentally, emotionally, or physically to dictate or block you from seeing the power that you have to change your circumstances. Frustration, despair, anger, agitation, and anxiety are all like the check engine light that comes on in the car and lets you know that something is wrong. Some ignore this light and end up with more issues down the road; the wise take it to the shop and get it hooked up for diagnostics.

This deep look within is called soul searching. It's the ability to dig deep and make a conscious connection to understand and embrace the discomfort. In essence, it's making a decision to walk out of the sun and into the white heat of transformation. It's using the suffering to fuel the natural survival/overcoming spirit within. Once you make the decision to embrace the heat of pain and discomfort, the universe/higher power will assist you in the rest, not do it for you.

Let's take Calum for example. After he transformed his frustration into action and completed the road, what happened? The 'universe' paved it! Something amazing happens when we make a conscious choice and do the things within our power to change our circumstances; our thoughts have energy, that energy leaves us and goes out and links up with like-minded forces to bring to fruition our deepest desires. The first step is yours though, stepping in and staying in the white heat of discomfort is where we change.

Buddy and I had no power over the intake system. We couldn't change the fact that we had to leave all our belongings behind, we had to shave our heads or go to seg, and we couldn't change the crowded situation in the shower. Focusing our energy on things we can't control is a waste of emotional energy and is counterproductive. By focusing our energy on things within our control and transforming our frustrations into fuel, we were able to go through the intake process embracing the discomfort as motivation to never put our lives/freedom in another man's hands again, through change.

In society, we cannot change many things. The neighborhoods that we start in, the negative attitudes of our coworkers at work and at home, we cannot make our spouse be on the same page as us. What we can control, and have power over, is our perspective of the situation, our attitude, and the lessons we make up in our minds to take from the circumstance.

See, when we move, or switch jobs, or get a divorce just to avoid the discomfort of a situation, we miss out on the 'white heat' moments of transformation that change us from clay pots into porcelain. In these different situations, we find ourselves with the same results because our frustrations never lead to growth or skills in thinking that lead to the wisdom of solving problems. That tension/frustration are indications that something needs to change, not be avoided. Later in the book we will speak about when it's time to get out of a situation; leave a clay pot in the furnace too long and you'll ruin it, but the right amount of time will transform it.

Rainer N. Rilke said something very powerful when he said: "The purpose of life is to be defeated by greater and greater things."

Some people 'go' through life while others 'grow' through life. Defeats are a normal part of life but being defeated is a choice. Our defeats/things that defeats us should be greater, stronger, and more challenging than the last because of the growth and lessons involved. This wisdom that we gain is not only for us, but for the people that we become responsible for.

It's not about where we start out in life, it's about the mental attitudes that we choose to start with that make the difference in the end. Don't run from your pain and frustrations, let them transform you.

KEYS TO FREEDOM

Freedom means a lot of things to a lot of people; losing your physical freedom, in the form of incarceration has to be one of the most difficult. Coming into the intake process was a surreal experience, this is when you know it's real. The only people at this point who 'seemed' to know what was going on, are those who missed the lessons from their previous sentences and had to come back to prison.

My whole mentality going through this process was that of supreme focus. I didn't want to miss anything, and as long as the intake process seemed to be, I knew, I had to endure it to the end, despite all the uncertainties. Like most things in life, having a strong start sets the tone. I knew this would be important for the duration of my fifteen-year sentence.

There will always be things in life we aren't prepared for, but, by opening your mind and focusing on the now—the things you can control—your perspective and attitude towards new experiences, you can set yourself up to meet any future challenges and be successful.

Year #2: Celly

You been going through the intake process all day. You're tired, you feel exposed, you're on edge, and frustration is a new tenant in your mind.

UCC (unit classification committee) is made up of mostly ranking officials such as one major, head of UCC, the records supervisor, and a lieutenant. This committee will give you an interview that will determine your job and what wings you go to. They ask your job skills as if they are going to consider placing you where you want to go, knowing they will only put you where they need you. Very few people end up in the jobs they ask for, most end up going straight to the field squad chopping down weeds, rocks, and grass with a hoe. This job assignment is the closest thing to old-time slavery. Slavery was meant to strip the slave of his identity through brute domination and repetitive subjugation to his position. Here in Texas, guards sit atop horses with cowboy hats and loaded shotguns and stare down upon you as you swing a hoe back and forth. This job assignment is meant again to break you mentally and reinforce the idea that you are no longer an individual, you are property, a number, an 'offender.'

You will leave UCC with your wing and cell location written on a slip of paper. A laundry boss and a few laundry workers will hand you a mattress full of lumpy wool and two sheets, if it's the winter months, then you'll also be handed a blanket.

With your property in one hand and mattress in the other, you will follow an officer to your wing. As you walk down the run (hallway) towards your new residence, your eyes are open to the hustle and bustle of prison life. Guards are yelling orders, directing traffic for school and chow time (breakfast, lunch, or dinnertime), dudes are nodding their heads saying, "what's up," and you're just trying to keep up so that you can go get settled in.

Finally, you make it onto the wing and your standing on one row with the dayroom to your right and about twenty cells right in front of you down a long corridor.

You nod 'what up' to a few dudes that greet you, you looking to see if you know somebody from your 'hood. You look down at the slip of paper and see you live on three row '316.' The guard tells you to go up to three row and then go down 16 cells and wait until the cell opens and then close the door behind you. You walk down to 316 cell and sit your things down and wait for the cell door to roll open. You look through the small holes and into the cell and you notice someone sitting on the bottom bunk. You look back down at the slip of paper and you see it says "316T" and you assume that the 'T' stands for top since the dude in the cell is already situated on the bottom bunk. Finally, you see a guard appear at the end of the run. The guard opens a panel and pushes a few buttons and your cell door rolls open. You step in, sit your stuff on the top bunk, and then close the cell door. It's just you and your 'celly.' The 'size-up' game begins.

This 'new world,' wide-eyed, tension dynamic is played out in the free world (society) also. We can remember the anxiousness of the first day of school where we didn't know anyone and being sized up by the clothes we had on or if our shoes were the newest sneakers that had just come out. We find this dynamic walking into the office of a new job and being the new man/woman on the crew and having to take in the energy of the environment at light speed and adapt as fast as possible while at the same time dealing with everyone's individual personalities. Even in our personal lives, while out on a date with our new love interest, we are 'sized-up' based on past accomplishments. Being sized-up is just part of our everyday lives.

Back in the cell, as you and your celly 'what up' each other and shake hands for the first time, everything is being taken in about the energy that you give off. Your tone of voice is analyzed in order to detect fear, self-doubt, nervousness, and uncertainty. As your new celly stood up to shake your hand he tested the firmness of your inner strength and it was noticed if you gave eye to eye contact during the handshake. Your height and weight are guessed and within a minute, your celly knows if he thinks he can whoop you or not.

All of the unspoken information that has been taken in will be used to set the 'tone' of the cell dynamic. There isn't a talk where one person comes out and says, "Now I am the Alpha! As long as you stay out of my way, you good homie." Based on Buddy's personal experiences we have noticed two predominate energy levels play out between cellies.

The first energy level that we both have commonly encountered based off the sheer strength of our natural character is one of 'mutual respect.' You shake hands with your celly and all of the non-verbal info has been gathered and he sits on his bunk and asks you to take a load off and have a seat on the toilet so that y'all can chop it up (talk). Y'all talk about everything from where y'all are from, to the ins and outs of the unit. A good celly will lace you up on what to listen for over the intercom and what certain things mean, and he will tell you who the 'good' guards are versus the bad ones. The most important aspect of this conversation is to establish 'cell time.'

The cell time dynamic is one of the biggest issues that most cellys have disagreements over. Because privacy is so scarce, having time alone in the cell is vital. You have been stripped of everything, your mind is all over the place, and sometimes you just need time alone to think or even to cry, and to 'release' built up tension (smile). If the right balance of cell time based on schedules can be worked out, then mostly everything else such as cleanliness and overall trust will work themselves out. With the right celly to start off your time, a lot of the stress and confusion of this new world can be eliminated.

The second dynamic is not so peaceful and it's a 'vibe of tension.' The most common issue from our experience is the tension between two alphas who can't agree over cell time. In this situation, one of the cellys has no job and hates going to the dayroom and so he stays inside the cell for most of the day, leaving the other celly with no time alone to think or handle private business. Inside the cell, the tension is thick, hardly no words are spoken, and things can go sideways at any moment.

Shallow conversation to fix things resolve the tension for a while, but in a few days' time, things go back to how they were. Now arguments erupt over small things and you stay on edge. The tension affects your rest, things are building up emotionally because there is no time to meditate to yourself, you feel drained at school, and you know (lock-up/seg) over a fight could be your reality any day. Buddy and I both have been through bad cellys and it's hell on the mental and emotional energy needed to minimize doing time.

We see this low mental and emotional energy at work in society when the people in our close proximity create an environment of tension. At our jobs, the envious co-worker is always on the lookout for an opportunity to sabotage you and your work; and so you are always on the mental defense and it takes away from the mental and emotional needed for creativity.

Our spouse is supposed to be like a cellphone charger to our souls. We are drained out in the 'world' trying to make it, striving to stay afloat in a competitive and cutthroat world. We come home drained and tired, ready to 'connect' to our life partner for uplifting, motivation, and hope, but instead we are drained with questions that reek of trust issues, doubt, and selfishness. Starting the next day off with a low mental and emotional charge, our social 'signals' are weak, and we can hardly 'connect' to the people and projects that are important to us. This goes to show that the people whom we allow access to our mental and emotional energy need to be individuals who understand and appreciate the power they hold.

One day I was in one of my college prep classes and my teacher always chose a 'word for the day' for us, as a class, to discuss. The word for that day was 'tact.' I opened the dictionary I had nearby and learned that it meant "having the ability to appreciate the delicacy of a situation and do or say the kindest or most fitting thing." As the class discussed different meanings, I was in deep thought thinking about how this word applied to my personal life, especially the current celly situation I was facing at the time.

I didn't know that it took "ability" to know that a situation was "delicate." This definition seemed to suggest that being able to recognize a sensitive circumstance had to be intentional. I had been going into situations with only my needs on my mind and not considering how my mindset was adding to the tension. Next, this definition sparked a thought and a new revelation that I had the power to do or say something that could change a delicate situation into a stable one. In that moment, I learned that I played an important part of the outcome of every situation in my life and moving forward, I would remain conscious of that power.

That night as the guards 'racked up' (put everyone inside their cells for the night) the wing I sat on the toilet (also used as a seat) and waited on my celly to come in. As my celly walked into the cell and closed it behind him, I was intently aware of how delicate the situation was and how it got that way. We both had focused on 'our' time in the cell, but on a deeper level, I saw that 'power' was at the root of our struggle. To give in would be to give up the perceived power that we both felt we had. The "ability to appreciate the delicacy," was the ability to look within any situation to the root cause. I had found it in ours.

He sat down on his bunk and I started the conversation. "Look bro, we been bumping heads for a couple of months now over cell time. We both alpha males and we use to setting the stage and our cellys making their schedules around ours without having to communicate or figure shit out. If things keep going the way they going, the inevitable going to happen and we got a lot to lose. Let's put our pride to the side, put our heads together and figure this shit out, bro."

He sat quiet for a minute in deep thought. I imagined the pride and egotistical rush moving through his blood now that I'd acknowledged his status as an alpha, his defensive wall falling. We locked eyes as he looked up from thought, he extended his hand. I shook it. "Yea bro, we been trippin'," he said, "you right we both got a lot to lose and we need to figure out some type of schedule that fits the both of us." That morning we came up with a schedule and we never had a cloud of tension in our cell again. That night I slept like a baby, I was well rested and focused at school the next day, and my irritability was now gone. Tact became a part of my life and way of thinking.

Richard Hooker said that, "change is not made without inconvenience, even from worse to better." This truth made since after reflection upon how tact became a way of life for me.

Not all situations can be fixed with tact. My co-author and friend, Walker (Buddy) learned this lesson through tribulation.

Sam was a three-time loser who knew the ins and outs of prison life, one of those dudes who think they know everything just because they have lived more years than you. Sam worked in the kitchen as a 3rd shift grill cook, a position he used to mask his true insecurities. Sam was Buddy's celly.

Inside the cell, Sam and Buddy hardly even spoke to one another and every time they did, it seemed to become a battle of wit that ended up in high tension and frustration. Because Buddy was young and ambitious, the inferiority complex that Sam already had residing in his mind was restless. This dynamic had Buddy restless and on edge, too.

One day Sam got off work and Buddy was in the cell drawing. The cell door opened, and Buddy could tell by the way Sam slammed the cell door that he 'was in his feeling' (moody).

Sam was quiet for a moment and then said, "Damn, you can't draw in the dayroom, nigga?"

Buddy, at the end of his rope exploded, "You can't tell me shit, what's up!" Buddy stood to his feet as adrenaline prepared him for whatever was next.

They stood looking into each other's eyes for a sec until Buddy said, "I ain't about to crash with you over no small shit, nigga, but this shit ain't gone work."

The next day Buddy kept his eyes open and noticed Sam in the dayroom having a meeting with his 'blood' homies. Every so often, different members would glance over at Buddy. Buddy knew what was coming next. Sam was a coward one on one, but with his homies, all of a sudden, he had courage. Buddy knew that if things didn't change soon, he would end up hurting someone or vice versa. He had tried to talk, compromise, and just ignore Sam and nothing had changed. It was time to think for the both of them.

That next morning during chow time, Buddy spoke to a lieutenant who was understanding, "Ma'am, I'm in school. I have very few minor cases, and I enjoy not seeing my family through a glass window at visit. I'm tryin' to keep things this way and if I'm not moved out of the cell that I'm in now, I fear, I'm going to do something I will regret later. Can you please do something to get me moved?"

The Lt., with no questions, picked up the phone, asked Buddy his cell number, and nodded her head that it was handled. Buddy said thanks and walked off, but nothing had happened. In the end, Sam was the one who ended up getting himself moved, but what we want to highlight is that it's okay to 'leave while you are ahead.' A situation that is threatening everything you've worked hard for isn't worth going backwards.

Socrates said, "let him that would move the world, first move himself."

If we are still moved by pure emotion and not by logic, we will never be in control of ourselves. Part of tact is 'doing' the most fitting thing in any given situation. Leaving the situation with your life, freedom, and peace of mind should always be the most fitting thing.

In Proverbs, the scripture says that, "Pride comes before destruction." Countless individuals in society have stayed in toxic situations that ended in tragedy and death.

At a certain job an individual stays in a toxic environment that is causing mental and emotional stress. This stress effects the person's work relations and performance. The person is fired, and in a fit of rage, comes back up to the job and shoots innocent people. With tact and wisdom, this individual could have easily asked to be transferred to a different location, or even found a new job. Pride should not get in the way of walking away from a toxic situation.

We see this dynamic play out in marriage and relationships over and over again. The love is gone, fighting is a daily occurrence, therapy didn't work, and intimacy is all but gone. Instead of leaving the bond as friends with a mutual understanding that things are over, one night a fight goes too far, and things turn for the worst.

A 'celly' is a person or people who have a direct influence over the energy of your environment which, in turn, affects your mindset and personal energy. In Robert Greene's book, *Mastery*, he speaks about the "seven deadly realities," and how to be on the lookout for these issues when dealing with those around us. Things like envy, conformism, rigidity, self-obsessiveness, laziness, flightiness, and passive-aggression. Without wisdom and tact, these realities can be constant roadblocks to our mental and emotional energy. When we're not thinking clearly, we're not acting clearly, and the results speak for themselves.

We once read a book by Dale Carnegie called *How to win friends and influence people,* and we took a key life principle that we live by and apply to our daily lives. In short, the principle says to imagine that everyone that you encounter has a sign around their neck that says, 'make me feel special.'

See, in a river or an ocean, it's the undercurrent that drowns most people who end up losing their lives while swimming. Even expert swimmers meet this fate when they don't respect the power of an undercurrent.

The skill of tact is the ability to see the sign around the necks of the people we encounter in any situation and make them feel valued and important. The ability to see their need. When we can't see the undercurrents of need and desire within individuals we live and work around, we end up being drowned with their envy, their passive-aggression, and self-obsessiveness. Instead of the flow of progress, we swim upstream fighting against other people's need to be validated and recognized.

When someone knows that you care, when they know that their needs are important, and you are shown in 'action' a willingness to help them, they will turn through the 'law of reciprocation' to help you meet your needs.

But, we all know of people who, no matter how much we try to compromise or show them that their needs are valid, or we are tactful as we know how to be, they still, for whatever reason, choose to be difficult. Draining our emotional energy seems to fuel them and they seem hellbent on getting in the way of where we are tryin' to go. These are the people that we must distance ourselves form. This reality can be very hard when the person that we must distance ourselves from is someone who has an emotional hold connection to our soul (mind, will, and emotions).

A wise man once said that, "Some think it's holding on that makes one strong, sometimes it's letting go." A wife, friend, or family member may continuously use 'emotional blackmail' (fear, obligation, and guilt) in order to keep us in a cycle of emotional and mental abuse. This "F.O.G" makes it hard for us to 'see' the effects that their behavior is having on us. We keep chasing a time when they were different, and sometimes we even find a way to blame ourselves for how they make us feel.

This cycle won't ever stop until we start to value our peace and stand up for what we deserve when it comes to our mental and emotional energy.

I know this cycle too well. I came from streets, and when I was living in the streets, I treated my then-girlfriend with little to no value. I hurt her in many ways. I came into prison and over the course of many years through willpower and determination, I transformed myself with the help of my higher power.

The same girl that I mistreated in the streets became my wife after me convincing her that I was different and changed, a new man.

What I didn't know was that if was my turn to be mistreated and hurt and treated with little or no value. I dealt with emotional abuse for over five years and as a man, it's hard for me to admit it. There would be times I would hang up the phone and go to my bunk feeling less of a man for the way I was allowing this woman to treat me.

At the time, I believed that "love was patient, love was kind, and held no records of wrong" meant that if you just put up with the abuse long enough, then a person would just change and 'love' would heal them. What I learned is that when you 'allow' someone to abuse you, not only do they lose respect for you, deep down you start to resent and lose respect for who they are.

I dug deep within and admitted to myself that I was being emotionally abused, this was a hard step. Then I made a vow to myself to never allow guilt or fear to subject me to any kind of abuse again. Then I started to stand up for myself first in a 'loving' manner, then things got nasty and the level of disrespecting one another got to an unacceptable level and divorce was the climax.

Robert Heinlein said something about love that made a lot of sense, "Love is that condition in which the happiness of another person is essential to your own."

I feel that this quote holds the key to thinking that should permeate our minds in all dealings involving 'cellys' of all kinds. If we learn the power to make another feel happy important, valued, and understood, then in turn others will be more prone to make us feel the same way.

KEYS TO FREEDOM

It wasn't until I got incarcerated that I began to understand the importance of negative energy. Unlike free society, you cannot just leave negative interactions. With people in prison there are so many different personalities and attitudes in a small area that in order to survive, and even thrive, you must learn to read people and their intentions.

At the base of understanding people is understanding and reading yourself. This begins with self-awareness. In order to understand people at their heart, mind, and emotions, you have to understand your own. This starts out as being realistic as possible about who you are, your emotions, fears, and beliefs toward life. By understanding yourself, you can begin to empathize with others in your environment whether you're in prison or free society.

With this new perspective in life you can then begin to navigate through encounters with people and be more effective in your daily interactions. Each person will become a new experience, and this will shape your perspective in life and the people you deal with.

YEAR # 3 INMATE.COM

Wright in 1989 and Tannen in 1990 both came to the conclusion through study and experimentation that women take pleasure in conversing face to face and use this dynamic to explore potential relationships, while men enjoy 'doing' things together and use communication to come up with solutions. They must not have done their study in prison cause 'Inmate.com' spreads more confusion in prison than it does solutions.

In prison, the spread of information from person to person is not called 'the grapevine' but 'inmate.com.' This information source is present right from jump. In the intake process it's in the form of dudes telling you how not to answer certain questions about your family history and personal drug use, all the way to how someone heard that if you played crazy in a certain way you could get on psych meds with no trouble.

Based on who your 'celly' is, inmate.com comes in the form of him lacing you up on what female's 'good' to jack on (masturbate), all the way to who the 'punks' are and who snitchin'.

This information is taken in like a sponge in this new world because as humans, one of our number one needs is 'security.' Coming into this new world, you feel everything but secure and this information is the first thing that you end up holding onto in order to feel safe.

The danger and uniqueness of inmate.com is that it is made up of fact and fiction, rumor and truth, wisdom, and foolishness. A piece of information that starts off as a fact is not always presented as the truth, it changes and evolves as it grows into something that resembles little of what it started out as, sometimes with tragic consequences.

Like we said, this information is powerful because it serves as a form of mental security, but it also taps into the need for us as humas to conform to the 'norm' of our environment.

In 2009, in "The Empathy Instinct," primatologist Fran de Wall said, "When I see synchrony and mimicry—whether it concerns yawning, laughing, dancing, or aping, I see social connection and bonding." Taking in this information helps us with our nature as natural mimics.

Inmate.com has great influence on everything from how one spends his time and structures his day to his mental and mediational energy, and the future expectations he expects. For example, a bit of information may come down the line on inmate.com saying something like, 'Muhammad working tonight!' Everybody know that Muhammad 'police' everything and so in a scramble, everyone 'putting everything up,' getting your cell in order, and just being on point. Later on, you find out that he is working, but it's not on the wing but on perimeter check. You done made moves based on this information that sometimes can't be undone until the next day. You might have scheduled an appointment with the tat man and now that he done moved things around because of inmate.com, you have to reschedule. This example is of a minor nature, but as we get deeper in the chapter, we will show how inmate.com can have serious consequences.

Inmate.com is close cousins with 'social media' outlets such as Facebook and Twitter. Things get taken from social media and spread from person to person at a much faster rate than we've ever seen in history. As humans we are constantly defining and redefining our identity and who we are constantly is uniquely connected to the information that we adhere to. We are bombarded with information from every angle, vying for our attention, belief, and pocketbook. If we are not careful, we can find ourselves in dark places and even taken advantage of based off some of the misinformation that comes from society and social media. We definitely see the dark side of misinformation through stories like the one of the young college students whose friends decided to play a prank on him. While he was asleep, they had another man get into bed with him and lay next to him as if they were lovers. They took pictures and the next day posted them on social media for the world to see. Even though when things turned sideways his friends tried to tell everyone that the pics were a prank, a joke, the shame, and ridicule was just too much.

Not able to take it anymore, he took a pump shotgun from his dad's gun shed and ended his life. These are the deadly consequences of misinformation and social media. In prison we see this dynamic play out when a person gets the label of being a 'snitch' or a 'cluck' or even a 'punk.' Whether the information is true or not, once things are spread and reputations are ruined, sometimes a person's sense of self is ruined, too.

John Updike said it like this, "facts are generally overstated. For the most practical purpose, a thing is what men think it is. When they judged the earth flat, it was flat. As long as men thought slavery tolerable, tolerable it was."

This quote shows why social media and inmate.com hold so much power. All it takes is belief, not truth, to cause destruction. Some of the information that we gravitate towards is information that we already believe in a different form, such as ideas and values. This truism is most prevalent in the political arena and race relations.

When a person identifies with a certain political party and believes that this party represents who he/she is as a person and upholds the personal values that they adhere to then the 'spin' that a party puts on a situation will resonate with that individual most of the time without question. For example, at this time in America, racial tension is high due to police brutality towards minorities. Those on the Democratic side believe that the protests are vital and peaceful for the most part. On the Republican side, protests are mostly viewed as violent and disruptive. Because of the way each party paints the narrative, it effects the way people receive and perceive information.

It's a sad day in America when, based on party lines or the color of your skin, we find ways of thinking, instead of being able to look at any situation objectively and say what's right for all involved in a balanced manner. Even when we feel conflicted by a situation, it's hard for some to let go of the comfort old ideas and ways of thinking give.

People hold onto old and false information for different reasons.

My co-author, Buddy, seen this truth when it came to the inmate.com lie/rumor about the 'One-Third Law.' This is one of the biggest myths that has passed down the inmate.com pipeline. This law says that a person in prison will only have to do one-third of his sentence before he is eligible to see parole. So, say I got a five-year sentence, under this law I would only have to pull 1 ½ years before seeing parole; if I have a twenty-year sentence, then I would only have to do 7 ½.

When this rumor hit the prison system, it sank its teeth in and refused to let go. It hit like a virus and infected the minds and hopes of many men. Like I mentioned up top, a fact is not always presented as the truth. The fact of the one-third law was that it was a bill that had been presented/introduced as legislation, but it had never 'passed' as the rumor through inmate.com had suggested.

Buddy met this dude named Juvi who was about forty years old with a fifty-year sentence. They called him 'Juvi' because he had come to prison as a youngster and had basically grew up in the pen.

When a man has been gone as long as Juvi, on a subconscious level he looks for anything to distract him from the reality of his situation. Unknown to him, he was always on the lookout for the 'next distraction', when the one-third virus made its way into his system, it took over. Everywhere he went he spread the news that he was about to go home, he was excited, and even his walk was different. He had a renewed hope that you could see in his eyes.

One day, in the dayroom, Juvi came across Buddy with this news of him going home. "it's ova wit Buddy for ya boy, you gon look up soon and wonder where I'm at." Juvi said with a smile.

Buddy said, "Oh, you seen them people? What they give you?" Juvi pulled out a piece of paper from a folder and showed Buddy a passage saying that the law had passed. "See boy, I know soon as they get around to my case, I'm gone," he said with excitement. Buddy slid the paper across the dayroom table and took a closer look for himself. After close examination, he noticed that the page was printed from someone's personal blog and not from an official website run by the State of Texas.

"I hate to tell you, but this from a blog bro, this somebody opinion; this ain't fact," Buddy said.

"My sister sent me this bro, she ain't gone send me nothing that ain't official. Why you being negative bro, they passed the law, niggas always hatin'," Juvi said in frustration.

"I'm just tryna save you some heartache and disappointment, bro, believe what you want to believe, that's on you," Buddy said.

Juvi walked away from the conversation with a mug on his face convinced that Buddy was just a hater trying to steal his joy. About two months later, Juvi approached buddy in the dayroom while he was chilling, "say bro, that shit that my sister sent me, and these other niggas was saying was true was bogus. I should have heard you out. Next time I ain't believing shit that ain't verified through a reliable source, or that I haven't studied myself." Juvi said what he had to say and then walked off.

There is a quote that says, "A faith that cannot survive collision with the truth is not worth many regrets" –Arthur Clarke

Juvi needed to believe, just as a heroin addict knows that his fix will end in sickness, Juvi needed his fix, no matter the possible mental and emotional anguish in the end in sickness, feeding our hope and verifying our established beliefs is the food that inmate.com and social media feed on. This is why these information sources are, at times, so dangerous.

Buddy witnessed the despair in Juvi's eyes as he explained the hard lesson, he had learned from believing the unestablished 'truths' his desire caused him to believe. Buddy being the type who can learn from other's pain, this experience motivated him in his own life to slow down when it came to believing things that feel natural to believe, things that seem to feed something deep within. He vowed and made a new commitment to verify information before standing on it as fact. Choosing to make this lesson a lifestyle has saved him a lot of heartache and frustration.

In his book *The Road Less Traveled*, Scott Beck calls this lesson being "dedicated to reality." He says, quote, "We are daily bombarded with new information as to the nature of reality. If we are to incorporate this information, we must continually revise our maps, and sometimes when enough new information has accumulated, we must make very major revisions. The process of making revisions, particularly major revisions, is painful, sometimes excruciatingly painful. And herein lies the major source of many of the ills of mankind…"

I agree with Scott when he states that "only a relative and fortunate few continue until the moment of death exploring the mystery of reality, ever enlarging and refining and redefining their understanding of the world and what is true…" Juvi, Buddy, and myself are a part of the few who have made the decision to, no matter how painful it may be to protect ourself from the stagnation of 'mental growth' when it comes to what is truth and what is not. This mindset is a lifestyle that is constant and the moment one lets his/her guard down, 'fantasy' can become our reality.

I remember coming into the prison system and seeing firsthand the power of inmate.com. Just like Buddy, I, myself also learned a valuable lesson from another person's pain. When you 'fall out of place' in prison you are usually going to another wing/dorm in order to handle some quick business during mass movement. Falling out of place on your wing is mostly when you enter another person's cell during count time while the real person stays in the dayroom and says your cell number. The count will show that both of y'all are accounted for, this is really all TDCJ cares about. When you fall out of place on your wing it's mostly for tats and other business; sometimes homosexuals pull this move in order to get some private time together.

Jason was the tat man on this particular wing and at this time about three times a month, he was having a known homosexual falling out of place into his cell. According to Jason's version, the homosexual that he was doing work on stubbed his toes on the toilet, which caused him to 'walk funny' one day when he was coming out of Jason's cell.

Others on the wing saw it different and the word spread that Jason 'had the punk limping' coming out of his cell. Not only did this tarnish his rep, but he lost all business because the 'punk' was rumored to have HIV, so people were fearing that his tat gun was contaminated. Within a month, word that Jason was a 'punk' was all over the unit. With his name tarnished and no way of making money, he spent more time in his cell isolated. This caused him and his celly to start having issues. One day during count, an officer, upon walking past Jason's cell, noticed his limp body lying on the floor. He called over the radio for help. The nurses pronounced him dead on arrival from a pill overdose.

That night laying on my bunk, I was contemplating what must have been going through Jason's (not his real name) mind when he decided to take his life. How could it have gotten that bad in his head? I just didn't understand. William Shakespeare, in 1599 said, "But life, being weary of these worldly bars, never lacks power to dismiss itself." Right then I made a vow that before I spoke or spread something, I would verify that it was uplifting and inspirational. I made a decision to never allow a negative rumor to pass through my lips; also, to never lend my ear to a gossip. Sir Phillip Sidney passed some game to me about that. He said, "whoever will gossip to you, will gossip about you."

We do as much damage when listening to a gossip as when we spread what they say. Me, I chose to uplift and spread those things that would make a difference in a person's life, things that give hope and motivate. When someone come to me on some gossip dish, I'm direct to the point, "Straight up bro, I don't' gossip, and don't' entertain it either. Go talk to him (the person they are talking about) about that like a man." This is a way of life for me and my boy, Buddy.

In psychology, 'informational social influence' is defined as "Influence resulting from one's willingness to accept others' opinions about reality." That trait is under the family of different kinds of conformity. This and other types of conformity are a normal part of social order and will always be a part of our lives. If you are heading into an event and you see everyone running in the opposite direction, I think it would be a safe bet to accept their reality that something isn't right. Find out later if you were wrong (smile). What we want to share with you from our experience here in prison is hope to set you free from falling into the misinformation trap.

When the 'fog' of misinformation comes rolling in doing its best to capture your mental and emotional energy, you must 'park your car' and allow the fog to clear before you drive on.

With misinformation from inmate.com, social media, and other platforms being the fog, the car is your mind and decisions you decide to make. Attempting to drive, fly, or even walk in thick fog has lead to many lives being lost and altered forever. When we say "park your car," we are asking that when a piece of information comes to you that is connected to a major part of your life/who you are, it's okay to just stop and allow time for mental processing and validation before acting on what was heard. Once the fog has cleared (you have validated and verified the information), you can then drive on knowing that you are making a clear-minded decision.

We all like to believe that we make decisions based on rational thinking and analysis when in reality, a lot of our evaluations and decisions are emotionally charged and based on information that is inaccurate. Slowing down and pausing allows us to 'think through' the cloud of emotion and tap into the rational side of our minds that leads us to wisdom and proactive decision making. That night, I lay back on my bed thinking about what Jason must have been going through emotionally, mentally, and even spiritually. And even though I made my mind not to even contribute to the destruction that rumors and false information cause I had to think deeper and find a way to prepare and protect myself from false info that could potentially be spread against me. How would I prepare myself not to be another Jason? I talked to Buddy about it and he gave me a quote by a lady named Rita May Brown, "about all you can do in life is be who you are. Some people will love you for you, most will love you for what you can do for them, and some won't like you at all."

Information that attacks your character, who you are as a person, and the respect that we all so rightfully desire, is especially challenging to deal with. Thinking about the quote by Miss Rita, the lesson that I learned that set me free from the potential deadly effects of misinformation against me is to 'love myself.' With that self-love as my foundation, I stand up for my respect. Any false information that may be spreading, I address it head-on and with authority! After that, people can believe what they want to believe. I get to the source and address it directly, clearing any misinformation up preventing its spread as much as I can (locus of control).

When it comes to information that's not so close to home as far as who you are, but can potentially affect your daily actions, mood, or say finances, it's important to be grounded and not 'easily influenced' like the wind moves the water. Take in the information and then use research, wisdom, and personal experience to make a clear determination as to whether the information can be used in a decision; especially information that you seem drawn to. My motto with information and even people is 'trust but verify' (smile).

We also want to remind you to spread information that is uplifting, motivating, and transformational. An individual's flaws need to be brought to them in a way that motivates them in growth. When you take these flaws to others behind their back in gossip, it adds to the person's issues, not helps them grow from them. Like grandma used to say, if you ain't got nothing good to say, don't say nothing at all.

In the third edition, *New College Dictionary* by Webster, the definition of information is "2. Knowledge derived from study, experience or its information that was studied, wisdom that you've gained through experience, or instruction from some that you trust."

KEYS TO FREEDOM

There's three forms of reality:

Subjective Reality.

Objective Reality.

Intersubjective reality.

Subjective reality starts with one's self, your thoughts, knowledge, and experiences.

Objective reality are things in nature and life that cannot be denied, life itself, and aspects of nature.

Lastly, there's intersubjective reality, the most powerful form of reality, because it plays on human nature, and the need to believe in things outside of self, i.e. God, religion, politics, and laws.

The majority of the world population has always chosen to go along with groupthink for many reasons. There has always been 'comfort' in numbers. How else could we explain American slavey and the German Holocaust? It wasn't until the media monster of the sixteen hundred spread the news of blacks being inferior to whites, that it became the norm to enslave Africans and that blacks were sub-human, therefore, bound to chattel slavery. Leading to 1933, where Adolf Hitler was named Chancellor of Germany, which led to the Holocaust where millions of Jews were murdered. Mass media and inmate.com has always controlled the collective mind state. What we are purposing here, is the return to subjective reality/you-think, instead of groupthink. Learn to think for yourself first, acquire knowledge and wisdom trough your own experiences; we can make better decisions that are tailored to our own lives. This is how we will become the individuals we were destined to become, and not mere sheep caught up in herd mentality!

YEAR #4: DAYROOM LIFE

If you are on the wing and not in your cell, then nine times out of ten your inside what prison calls the 'dayroom.' On any given day, you can look around the dayroom and see a melting pot of races, mostly black, Mexican, and white naturally segregated into their own sections. In older days, this segregation wasn't 'natural' based on just sitting by the people that you have the most in common with; it was 'forced' and intentional based on gang territory. Today, some units still enforce this way of life, but for the most part, people just naturally sit with the people they kick it with the most.

The dayroom is the place where one goes to meet up, play different board games such as Scrabble, dominoes, cards, and chess. This aspect of the dayroom has revealed to me the inner kid in alot of adults; not in the negative sense, but it's helped with a deeper awareness that we all need 'play' no matter how old we are.

The dayroom area is also where the television is located. On average there will only be two TVs in the dayroom. On most units there is an unwritten rule that one of the TVs is a sports television and the other is for shows and movies. The TV in the dayroom is one of the most conflict-causing aspects of prison that I have ever seen. Imagine twenty grown men sitting in front of one TV. Ten want to watch one show and the other ten want to watch something different. Sometimes a vote works, but most times the most dominant group wins out.

Depending on the culture of the dayroom/dorm you can find anything from dudes smoking different drugs off in the corner, dudes sipping on hooch, and some wings dudes 'jack off' on female guards working in what's called the rotunda. It's wild, but it happens depending on the culture of the environment.

Fresh into the system the influence inside the dayroom has some of the same effects in shaping who you become in prison, as much as your hood has on who you become in life, if you allow them to. Scientist define our environment as, "every nongenetic influence, from prenatal nutrition to the people and things around us." The fact that they use the word "influence" in their definition says a lot about the power of environment on how we see the world and our behaviors.

In 1955, in a study on conformity, Solomas Asch conducted an experiment in which he told students that they were going to be a part of a study on visual perception. In this study, students had to say which comparison line was equal to the standard line that was presented. In the first two trial runs, all five students guessed the same match to the standard line, but in the third trial, one student doesn't know that he is about to be tested on the power of conformity. Four of the students who answered before him answered the exact 'clear' wrong answer. The student sits up straighter in his seat and looks closer trying to see what everyone else is seeing that he doesn't. When he is finally asked his answer, he is hesitant and seems unsure about what to say. Asch's results were disturbing because he found that one-third of the time, these educated college students were willing to call "white, black" in order to conform to the group.

In prison when a dude enters the 'jack game' (masturbating on female guards), it's because they either observed someone doing it, or someone told them, "this is what it is over here homie, trust me, she good!"

See, the thing about conformity is that just like the students in Asch's experiment, even if in your heart you know something is 'wrong/not something you do,' in order to not feel incompetent, and not stand out from what the homies deem 'good,' they conform. For some, it's just an opportunity to express the perverse and barbaric desires of their soul (mind, will, and emotions).Scientist, preachers, and even shrinks understand that we as humans are pack animals that feed off the energy and influence of the group dynamic and this is why the 'pipeline' from the streets to prison has continued to thrive. Each generation follows the set examples left by the previous 'hood leaders' and the mindset motto is, "it is what it is." The definition for culture based on psychologists is, "the enduring behaviors, ideas, attitudes, values, and traditions shared by a group of people from one generation to the next."

The man who doesn't take in account for the power of environment is playing a dangerous game. The lies that we tell ourselves are the easiest ones to tell. Being mentally aware of the influential power of our peers and surroundings is vital in cultivating real change.

Mark Twain said something powerful that stuck out to us. He said, "whenever you find yourself on the side of the majority, it's time to pause and reflect."

When you first get the inkling that something is wrong with the way you are living your life, and you start to feel an uneasiness in your soul that you are living below the potential within you, one of the first steps to 'breaking free' from the old molds that have been set, is to do as Mark Twain said—"pause and reflect."

There has been a long-standing battle in science on what traits we are born into this world with versus what we pick up from the external experience of living. Back in the day, the Greek Plato (428-348 B.C.E.) believed that we came into this world with our intellectual abilities and even our character, while Aristotle (384-322 B.C.E.) believed that as we go through life, our experiences shape us. Today, scientists who study 'nature -vs- nurture' conclude that our makeup is a mix of both. Their saying is that, "nurture works on what nature endow" meaning that our environments and experiences will build off of our natural dispositions. In real life this means that a lot of prisoners who become drug addicts already have been 'passed down' a natural 'taste' for drugs, and those who go to excel and get college educations have been passed down a disposition for intelligence.

We feel that we are not slaves to either, but that at any moment you pause, reflect on our life and where you want to go, and then go create how you see yourself and the life you want. Period!

The cowbird is an excellent example of resisting the influences that we are born into. The cowbird is what scientists call a 'good parasite.' This means that they will scope out the nest of other birds for days and then when the coast is clear, the cowbird will fly in and lay eggs and then fly away. These birds have been known to lay up to 70 eggs a season in other nests. In most cases the 'foster mother' watches over the eggs as if she laid them, although in most cases, cowbird eggs are much larger than her own.

What scientists don't understand is how, when cowbird babies are born, they don't do as normal baby birds do and imprint. When young animals imprint, they follow and mimic the example of the first example they encounter (usually their mother). In watching the young cowbirds, scientist learned that they were resistant to the natural imprinting tendency. Upon closer observation, researchers came up with two reasons they felt that cowbird babies resisted imprinting. The first reason they guessed had to do with how the cowbird mother would sneak back into the nest and check on her chicks when the foster mother was away looking for food. The second thing that researchers noticed was that at about 22-28 days old, young cowbirds would sneak out of the nest to go socialize with others like themselves before returning back to the nest.

Up top, when I spoke about not being a slave to nature or nurture, the cowbird baby is an excellent example on action that we can take to 'resist' our natural inclination to follow the examples around us when we have the power to make choices. One, it's important to have a 'mother,' a positive role model, friend, coach, and teacher, who can check in with us on a regular basis to make sure we are on the right track.

Second, what we can learn from the cowbird and apply to our lives is the practice of surrounding ourselves with like-minded individuals who can hold us accountable and make sure we are living up to our potential. Sneaking out from the foster mother's nest and meeting up with other cowbirds allowed the baby cowbirds to connect with their true identity and also get a sense of direction. We all need these aspects.

Here in prison, Buddy and I both had help resisting the imprinting of the prison mindset from older wisemen who saw potential in us and helped us navigate through the different negative influences. Some of this direction came from others and some came from personal experiences.

One of these experiences came from the dayroom for Buddy. Coming into prison Buddy was determined to learn as much as he could about the black race, the history, and where we came from. In that study he came across information on Willie Lynch and the system he implemented on breaking and dividing slaves.

Upon entering the dayroom one day, Buddy saw an old-school man about sixty-five limping through the dayroom looking for a place to sit. Old-school finally found him a place to sit, but unbeknownst to him, the bench he decided to sit on 'belonged' to a gang. Not three minutes passed before Buddy witnessed a youngster tap School on his shoulder and ask him to get up.

"Say School, you can't sit right there, this a Crip bench and if you ain't crippin' then you slippin'," the youngster said.

Buddy was leaning against the wall just taking in the entire scene, amazed at how the lynch division was still in effect.

Old-school said, "Come on now youngster, ain't nobody even hardly in the dayroom, let Old-school make it." School just shook his head, got up slowly and went and found another seat.

Buddy was hot (angry) at the way the youngster had treated school and so he went and sat in the same seat the youngster had just forced School to move from. He was hoping the youngster would try him. Three minutes after he sat down, they called chowtime, and everyone left the dayroom.

Laying in his bunk that night, Buddy knew that fighting a physical battle wasn't going to solve the problem of division when it came to blacks in prison. He was frustrated that after all this time, slavery, and division, we were still operating with a 'slave mentality.' He loved his people but had lost respect for the 'nigger' mindset and ways of thinking. The incident with School showed him that even though we had lost our physical chains, some of us were still operating in our mental chains.

Buddy came across a quote by Jean Jacques that he agreed with. It said, "Slaves lose everything in their chains, even their desire of escaping from theirs."

Buddy could agree because prison had become the new modern-day plantation and the divide and conquer tactic was still in effect. This realization inspired Buddy to dig deeper into black history and soul-search deeper within himself, looking for any signs of lingering mindsets.

Instead of becoming a part of the system in that particular dayroom, Buddy used it to motivate himself to learn, grow, and then later, inspire others by teaching them where some of our 'divisive' actions come from and why we must come together.

For me, the dayroom experience and the influences that thrive within them were slightly different. Like most people in this world, I struggled with who I would be in prison. Who would I present to people, who should I present? In psychology, they say that the definition of self-concept is: All our thoughts and feelings about ourselves, in answer to the question, 'who am I?'

While internally I had decided to change and grow into something better in prison, outwardly I made a conscious decision to present an image that said, "I'm not to be messed with! Stay out of my way and I'll stay out of yours, period!" In thinking this way, I naturally gravitated towards actions that would reinforce this perception. When it came to the influence prisons had on getting tats (tattoos), I naturally fell into the trap.

In the dayroom one day, I observed a Mexican dude tatting and went over to him asking what was up on getting some 'work' done. One thing leads to another and before long I was getting a new tat every other week. Muscled-up with tats, this is the image I thought would send the message I wanted to portray.

In the later years of doing my time, after gaining much more wisdom and understanding about what true respect was and how one obtained it, I started to reanalyze my tats and getting them. I started to think about my future and where I was going and creating the image I knew lined up with the person I was internally. George Bernard Shaw said it this way, "Life isn't about finding yourself; life is about creating yourself." I decided never again to allow my environment to dictate who I should be or what I should present. Now I present who I am at all times and allow those in my environments to respond how they may. I understand now that it's not the perception that you give off that determines your level of respect, but your 'heart' and the way you carry yourself in your everyday actions. As my eyes opened to the true reality of prison, I seen dudes with tats and muscles that got treated like hoes, while the skinny dudes with no tats demand an aura of respect.

As people we are always growing, changing, and creating new 'selves' as we gain more wisdom and experience different things. When I think about the quote from George Bernard Shaw, it rings true because how can we find a self that is always changing? What I can say is we must find and define our core values and things that are important to us and then create who we are around those 'foundational things.' This way, as we transform and are influenced by things around us, our foundation is solid. So, when I say that 'I present who I am' at all times, in essence what I am saying is that my daily action lines up with my core values. (95% of the time, smile). As humans, we have the ability to present different parts of ourselves in different situations; this is what I believe Shaw meant when he spoke about creating yourself.

We would do you a great disservice if we underestimated the power and pull of your 'free world dayrooms.' We know that in order to feel normal at times we give into the 'norms' presented to us or we face constant frustration.

It's not lost on us that a lot of the choices that we make are motivated from external stimuli, and our position is not that external stimuli is negative. What we choose to highlight is the fact that if you are not careful, the influences that surround you can move you in a way that is unhealthy. If we are not careful, we can get lost in the 'systems' that we enter because we allow them to define who we are and where we are going. Although we acknowledge the fact that our environments are powerful, as we move through these influences, we have the power to take bits and pieces from these events and create a direction for our lives that fit our vision. This way we are shaping ourselves in a conscious manner, instead of allowing our 'dayrooms' to follow set patterns for us to follow.

As we live life, we experience new things, we meet new people, and we change the way we think. Adversity comes our way and the pain shows us something about ourselves that we didn't know, other trials and tribulations change the way we see the world. We see the world different when we have children than when we don't. In our parent's house the world takes on a different look than when we go to college and we are out there on our own. In essence, we grow from self to self, taking bits and pieces with us from our experience and creating the foundation that we stand on. Along this journey, part of ourselves die in order to make room for the birth of other selves. 'Lil-Cuzz' (my old gang name) died in the county jail along with my thirty-year sentence and gave birth to B.O.B. B.O.B. evolved into the 'KING' I am today.

Although we go through these phases and they are a part of life that we can't escape, our individuality is created and developed in these fires and self evolves out of this beautiful mess (smile). The events themselves don't' create us. If we are smart, we take the lessons from these events and use them as tools to shape the foundation that we stand on, then we are maximizing and 'growing' through life instead of 'going' through life.

Those who lack the vision it takes to shape their lives usually have the mindset of 'going with the flow.' It's much easier to allow our environments/dayrooms to 'think for us' and to follow the status quo instead of using those experiences to build on the process of, creating to the end, the self we will eventually become.

It's vital that during this journey called life, in order to evolve, we must stop along the way and pay attention to check engine lights that flash within, warning us that something is wrong and needs to be changed. These flashing lights come in the form of a lack of peace, and unsettling feeling in the soul, anxiety, and dissatisfaction. It's up to us to use soul-searching to dig deep and reveal what it is these emotions are trying to show us. Let's say for example I'm in a relationship/marriage and within my soul for some reason I'm not at peace and I keep getting the feeling that it's time for me to leave. In order for my new self to emerge, I must use with my soul is trying to show me and have the courage to break free from the marriage that is stealing my peace and emotional energy. Most would allow this environment to keep them stuck inside a dead situation, stagnated and unable to grow and move on to a better version of themselves.

When an environment/dayroom/circumstance is stealing your peace and emotional energy, your true self will whisper within and give you a sign that something has to change. You will know you have made the right decision when you change the circumstance and your peace returns and you added wisdom to your foundational values.

Buddy used his frustration to motivate him to dig deeper in his understanding of his people so that he could set them free. As for myself,

I used the tattoos as motivation to dig deeper, stop, and self-reflect.

Something strange starts to happen when you, as someone who is not afraid to be who you are, starts to stand on what you truly believe in. In some cases, you begin to change/influence those around you. Your 'dayroom' begins to change to the new vibe that you set as a leader. You have the power to set a new standard and give people courage to be who they really are instead of what has been shown to them. Like the baby cowbird you act as the like-minded siblings who they can fly to when they need to reconnect to the foundation of who they are. Emerson said something very powerful: "Do not go where the path may lead, go instead where there is no path and leave a trail."

We want to leave you with this, once you find out what is important to you and have the courage to stand on that foundation, show others the way. Instead of your environment influencing you, you influence your environment.

KEYS TO FREEDOM

It can be debated that our environment plays a crucial part of who we become. In life, with so many different influences for our attention in modern times, such as social media, entertainment, and pop culture, modern man and woman could easily be said to be by-products of the times. Although these platforms are nearly impossible to ignore in today's culture, it still doesn't make it impossible.

Every civilization has had its social norms and customs that the masses adhered to. In the Dark Ages, superstition prevailed in Europe for centuries. Devils, demons, and witches ran ramped in the collective mindset, although there was never any physical proof of these demonic entities. The collective mindset still nevertheless considered them real.

Although the majority believed in these superstitions, there were still a few people through plain uncommon sense that refused to believe in the fairy tales, these people were rational thinkers. Belief will always be a part of human nature, since we know this is fundamental fact of mankind. Choose to believe in yourself, stand on your personal foundational values, gained through experiential knowledge. So, when the dayrooms of life try to sway you, you can maintain your sense of direction.

YEAR #5 THE CELL

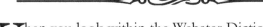

When you look within the Webster Dictionary and look up the word "cell," it's defined as, "a narrow, confining room." For our purpose here we are expanding the definition to mean, "anything that confines one's mental or physical movements." Although a physical cell is a place that is common in prison that keeps you locked in and locked out from society, a mental cell locks one into a place of fear and stagnation and keeps you from moving forward in your life.

In prison you walk into your cell and instantly you feel trapped. As soon as the lock engages on the cell door, you know that you have lost control of your movement and that choices are limited, as far as where you can go physically.

One of the first things you notice about a prison cell is that it is 'dark.' The dull dark gray walls have an energy and personality of their own that immediately has a pull on your energy. Some people, if their celly just happens not to be in the cell, sit their stuff down and break down in the darkness; the reality of their new life finally hitting home.

Another thing one notices about most cells in prison is the fact they have 'no windows.' With no windows, there is no occasional whiff of fresh air to remind you of the other side, no view of the trees and/ or birds flying to get your mind off the darkness of your reality. Your 'vision' is restricted, and you can't 'see' past your condition. When you can't see past your condition, all you can focus on is the dark walls before you.

Written on most cell walls are the written trails of those who have come before you. "lil-Paul was here, '09," or "Fuck all bitches," or "Jesus loves you, I don't," adorns the walls of these cells giving you a glimpse of the mental state of that individual at the time. At the back of the cell you notice a light bulb with a string hanging down and you pull the string, 'light.'

On average, most prison cells on Coffield Unit measure about 6' by 9'. No one that I know has actually measured a Coffield cell, but you can almost spread your arms out and touch each side of the cell at the same time.

With two grown-ass men inside the cell, it's almost impossible to get comfortable, which is the goal. A cell is designed to disrupt your comfort and remind you daily of where you are and what your new reality is. This is why most prison toilets are made of cold steel. As soon as you sit down to use the restroom, you first feel the cold, and this effects the whole process. Not only does the cold steel effect you, but you have another grown-ass man in the cell with you that has to smell what you are releasing. Most unwritten rules say that when you to go shit and your celly is in the cell, you must put 'a sheet up' for minimal privacy and you must 'drop one, flush one,' or flush every time you drop one.

As you begin to unpack your belongings and get situated, you realize that everything that you now own must fit inside of a small locker. Not only must it fit, everything must be properly stored, or a case is possible. You feel vulnerable because when you leave the cell and your celly stays behind, all of your family pictures, food, and hygiene are exposed if you haven't bought a lock.

One thing about being stuck in a cell is that you get a feeling of powerlessness. You feel helpless to change the dynamic of your situation and this mindset steals your peace and hope. In order to try to escape the limited view of the cell most men/women in prison buy themselves a 'peek mirror,' a small mirror glued to a makeshift handle. This mirror allows those engaged in contraband to watch out for the law (guards) and for those in the 'jack game,' it allows them to 'snipe' a female guard from a long distance.

For those in the world it would be like living inside of an apartment closet with another person. But, let's not think that a prison cell is the only type of cells that we find ourselves trapped in. For when we look deeper at life, we see that every day, all over the world, we find people trapped in mental and emotional cells. These cells stem from the traumas of childhood abuse and abandonment. The chains that were locked around their ankles they still drag around today. How many women do we see today who were abused by their fathers, or sexually taken advantage of, who still carry the scars and wounds on their soul? How many of us were told that we would "never amount to nothing," and in despair to feel like we were something, got in trouble trying to prove ourselves? What about the relational cells that confine us in dead-end relationships and marriages? We feel confined, abused, and unable to be ourselves.

We walk into our homes and feel the darkness surround us. Our big home feels like a 6 by 9 cell and we are afraid to be vulnerable with our spouse.

What about the occupational cells that confine us at work? They drain our mental energy, our supervisors feel like guards, and our work assignments limit our potential and keep us stuck in the rat race. This is why we say that a cell is anything that confines one's mental or physical movement. What is sad is that in a physical cell, you have to wait 'til a guard comes and unlocks the door before you can move forward. In our mental and emotional cells, it is us that holds the keys and keep ourselves stuck in these cages of pain and immobility. Yes, it is sad that we keep ourselves in these cages, but the beautiful thing is the fact that we hold the keys to our own freedom when it comes to these mental and emotional cells. We learned this truth from the physical cells of prison by transforming what the cell was designed for through inner perspective and strength.

The reality of our world is the fact that we cover these cages of pain in society with cars, money, relationships, work, and even drugs and alcohol. We use these distractions the same way a prisoner uses a peep mirror to focus on everything else but the cell.

James Webster said something profound that stuck with us. He said, "We think caged birds sing, when indeed they cry."

From the outside, our marriage may look happy, the money that we flaunt around may seem to have us on top of the world; the executive, top-level job may seem to have us at peace, but a lot of these things are mere distractions from our cages within, a way to keep us seemingly smiling on the outside. But, in reality, we are crying on the inside.

There is hope inside of our cells! From our cells in prison, and from spending the time in the darkness and frustration, we have found the keys of using our cells to motivate us to change things. Then, using our mental transformations to transform our cells.

It's never the cells that confine us, it is our confining mentalities that keep us stuck and limited. Within the darkness of the cells, if you look deep enough, you will see the light. Ralph Waldo Emerson said it best, "When it is dark enough, you can see the stars."

My co-author, and close friend, Buddy knows about the darkness all too well.

As we said earlier, Buddy entered the street life. He made up his mind that he would rather die trying to be financially free than to work his entire life inside of the rat race and still end up a slave to the system of taxes and labor in the end.

As those who live the street life know all too well, when you're at the top of your game, your light shines bright for all to see. Those who notice your light the most are those who are the hungriest and want a piece of the pie that you eating on. Buddy found this fact out firsthand with the case he ended up coming to prison on. Some hungry dudes allowed their appetite for money to override their logic, called Buddy over to make a deal, and within the week the two individuals had lost their lives and Buddy was facing a capital murder charge.

Imagine the darkness that attempted to capture Buddy's mind at the time. This was his first time being arrested, he had never even seen the inside of county jail before, and now here he was, facing something that could take away the rest of his life. Upon entering the county for the first time, Buddy was immediately thrown in seg because of the level of his charge. This was the first time in his entire life that it was just him and his own mind, no distractions. On top of the gravity of his life being on the line, the love of his life was acting very distant at visits, as if she had already given up. The look in her eyes told Buddy all he needed to know, she left that last visit and his life. He was devastated. After all he given her in the streets, not only had the streets turned its back on him, but now his girl had done the same. The darkness was heavy in his 'cell.' All the so-called friends and family who had been in his face were now gone, so was his freedom. The only thing that was left was his voice. All his life he had listened to peer pressure, to his family about who and what he should be, and also the streets. Now, for the first time, he only had his voice to define who he was and what he was supposed to be.

Night after night as he laid in the darkness of his cell, all around him he heard hopelessness. At night, if you listened hard enough, you could hear grown men trying to stifle their tears; in the conversations that were going on, you could hear the hopelessness, the lack of vision, and the despair. Their hopelessness became contagious and started to take Buddy into the depths of darkness.

Buddy lost hope in who he really was. Striped of everything, it was hard to say what his identity was. He felt powerless of what could be done about his situation and he worried if he would ever see the outside world again. There was no escaping these thoughts, no weed to numb the pain. Buddy caved to the pressure and gave up mentally and emotionally. He longed for just a glimpse of the sunlight, a brief smell of some fresh air. He missed how grass looked blowing in the wind, but all he had was the dull light of his cell. With nothing to remind him of some form of hope, Buddy hit an all-time low.

One night when the darkness, mental and emotional anguish, was just heavy, Buddy swallowed a handful of pills in an attempt to escape the pain forever. As he sat on the floor, going in and out of consciousness, he could actually feel his body dying. This dying feeling was worse than the darkness that had led to him taking the pills. Buddy got scared. He was afraid to die by himself, all alone in a cell. His mother's face flashed in his mind, "How will she take the news?" He thought about his brothers and sister and what they would remember about their bro, the message he would be sending through his suicide. As tears rolled down his face, his life flashed and he saw all the things that he had already survived as a kid, the strength his mother had shown through the many trials and tribulations that life had thrown at her. Buddy got mad! All these examples he had of strength and perseverance and here he was, instead of looking the darkness in the eyes and learning, he was trying to end it all in fear.

He dug deep and fought the effects of the pills all night, his will power fighting against the pills caused him to rock back and forth for hours. At some point in the night, he must of fell over into sleep because, when he awoke the next morning, he was still on the floor.

He had beat death! This darkness had shown him his true strength! In that early morning, he made a decision to always use the darkness of his pain as a tool of growth and self-reflection. Just as a farmer uses dung and a weightlifter uses the pain of weights to transform, he would, for the rest of his life, use trials and tribulations to grow from. If he could beat death, he could beat anything!

With this new perspective, his cell wasn't as dark as it seemed just the day before. He drowned out the hopeless conversations around him and transformed his cell first into a temple. He began to meditate and soul-search on the examples of strength that he had within his subconscious and use their examples as lessons. He defined who he was and where he wanted to go in life and made up his mind that nothing would ever get in his way. If death couldn't stop him, what could? Next, he turned his cell into a gym. For a couple of hours every day he did push-ups, core exercises, and cardio. His cell also became a university where he began to escape into new worlds through reading and learning about things he never knew or understood. In his studies, he ran across two profound quotes that stood out to him. One is by Walt Whitman and it says, "Either define the moment or the moment will define you." The other is by Nikos Kazantzakis and it said, "The real meaning of enlightenment is to gaze with undimmed eyes on all the darkness."

Together these two quotes became a foundational truth that Buddy continues to live by. Never does he run from the darkness, but in every challenge, every pain, trial, heartache, struggle, or tribulation, he looks upon it with undimmed eyes and defines what the lesson is. He then turns that lesson into a principle that he stands on, not only for himself, but for those around him.

This is what we desire to share with you about the many different cells that seem to have us stuck and trapped. If within the darkness of your cells you would open your eyes and embrace the struggle, attempting to grow form it, you would start to see a glimmer of your true strength , like a distant star shining far off in the night sky. That light is the key that will unlock your potential to transform the way you look at who you are and the way you see your circumstances.

Buddy made it out of seg and back into population only to find his way back into seg. He bought his own T.V., had all the books he could read, and didn't have to deal with the negative drama of other individuals who had a lack of vision. The very place that almost swallowed him whole, the darkness that caused him to dig deep within, had now become his comfort.

When we spoke about the layout of the prison cell earlier, we spoke about the light at the back of the cell. Usually there is a string hanging from the light that you have to pull in order for the light to come on. The darkness of the cell motivates you to pull the string in order for you to see clearly and get everything in order.

In the midst of the darkness and despair of our lives, deep at the back of our minds, there is a string that needs to be pulled and it's the darkness that motivates us to reach out towards the string so that we can see clearly.

If we are honest with ourselves, it is in the darkest moments of our lives that we have grown the most. If this is a true statement, then more of us need to be walking towards our issues rather than away from them. It's clearly evident that the keys to freedom are within the struggles. But, as humans, we don't want to struggle, we don't' want the conflict, the deep soul-searching that it takes in order for us to solve our deepest issues. We would rather avoid them in hopes that they will just go away or get high to escape.

When we slow down and look at the great leaders that came before us, we will notice a constant pattern with them: Most went to a 'dark' quiet place in order to dig deep within for the answers.

When we look closely at the life of Buddha and his desire to achieve Nirvana through enlightenment, we see that at first, he tried fasting as a way to enlightenment. He fasted to the point where only skin and bone remained. He said that trying to reach enlightenment in this way was like "trying to tie the air in knots." He said, "This is not the way to passionless-ness, nor perfect knowledge, nor liberation…" What, then, did Buddha do? He got him something to eat and went into his dark place under a tree, resolved not to move until the answer to enlightenment were found. Because of this, the tree in Buddhism is called the Bodhi (enlightenment) or the bo-tree. There is something about these dark places of ourselves that present us with the opportunity to dig deep and pull on the strings of our soul for light. Before speaking about Jesus and his dark place, I want to point out a comparison/reality that both Buddha and Jesus faced while in their dark place.

While the Buddha was under the bo-tree, he was attacked and tempted by Mara, the spirit of evil. With Mara were his three sons: Confusion, Gaiety, and Pride, and his three daughters: Thirst, Delight, and Lust. When this attempt failed, Mara tried to get Buddha to go straight into Nirvana, which would save him from the burden of life. Buddha refused and didn't move from the tree until enlightenment came and he was ready to instruct and lead his disciples.

We see this comparison also in the life of Jesus. Jesus was led into his dark place, the wilderness, to test his strength after he received the Holy Spirit. He was led to fast but remained without food during the duration of his temptation.

While Jesus was in the wilderness, he was tested and tempted by the Devil, the spirit of evil, in three ways: First, the Devil asked Jesus to "turn a stone into bread," wanting him to give into the hunger of his flesh. Second, the Devil took Jesus upon a high mountain, showed him all the kingdoms, riches, and powers, and offered them to Jesus in return for worship. Lastly, the Devil tried to trick Jesus into killing himself by jumping off a high temple. In all three tests, Jesus stood on this foundational truth saying, it is written," referring back to the written work of God as his light.

What is evident is the fact that whatever this 'spirit of evil' is, it is still operating in dark places. When we look back at Buddy's story, we see that in the midst of the darkness, right before enlightenment, there is a test/attack that attempts to break your mind and take your life in either the physical or mental way. It's when we stay grounded and reaching to pull the string that turns on the light at the back of the cell that we are liberated and set free from our cages.

Another great leader that we want to highlight is Mohammed. Mohammed was greatly distressed about the condition of his people and the morale that was prevalent at the time. In order to gain clarity, he would enter a dark place, a cave, on many occasions on Mount Hira. Being weak from a lack of food, at times Mohammed would go into violent seizures and have visions. It is during one of these seizures that the Angel Gabriel appeared to him and gave him the revelation (enlightenment) he needed to liberate his people. Again, we see another great leader tormented with thoughts of doubts and suicide. He struggled to believe that the vision was real, and it was in this struggle that he almost gave into doubt. It wasn't until the Angel Gabriel had visited him a second time that he had the confidence and courage to move forward with the vision that he was entrusted with.

Buddha, a tree; Jesus, the wilderness; and Mohammed went into a cave; my co-author and I, a cell. The thing about these great leaders is that they didn't just find themselves in these dark places, they intentionally went into these places to find clarity and strength. This is a clear indication that the mental, emotional, and physical cells that surround us in our lives hold the keys to enlightenment.

If we look closely at the story from the Bible in Genesis about the beginning of time, we see that God didn't have to say, "let there be darkness." Darkness was the default setting of the world. But he did have to say, "Let there be light!" Our powers lie in knowing that darkness is just a byproduct of the absence of light. You can't turn on darkness, it will naturally show up in our lives where there is absence of light. It was in the darkness that God saw a need for light! This is the key: Your dark places will show you where your need for light is! Once you use darkness to see, you must speak light into your situation, pull the string at the back of the cell and watch the light of victory come on in your life.

A lot of people in their cells never make it to this point. Moody spoke about these types in his forward. Instead of using the darkness of the cell as a tool to show us where light is needed in our lives, some people just become one with the darkness and it takes their lives, not by force, but just as what we seen with Buddy, Buddha, Jesus, and Mohammed, it beckons, tempts, and tests hoping that you will give in with your own freewill.

Another great leader said something profound that we will conclude with. Mahatma Gandhi said, "The moment the slave resolves that he will no longer be a slave, his fetters fall, he frees himself, and shows the way to others. Freedom and slavery are mental states."

KEYS TO FREEDOM

Throughout history, great men and women have shared a common link. This link between them was a vision, the ability to see things around them and in themselves that others couldn't believe or see. Visions are powerful because in order to gain clarity in your vision, you must go through some form of adversity and through these dark times to gain the ability to see through the doubt, disbelief, and limitations of others around you.

Just because we gain the ability to see through the darkness doesn't mean our path through it loses its strength against us. No, by no means; things become even more difficult for us the closer we get to seeing our vision becoming a reality.

A Japanese proverb says, "Vision without action is a daydream; action without vision is a nightmare."

Having a vision doesn't mean anything if we aren't putting the work behind it and putting in work without the vision is essentially doing nothing because our heart isn't in it. Even in the midst of life cells, see your vision through. This will be the result of a focused mind.

YEAR #6: WORK CALL

In prison, there is a saying that says, "The penitentiary gone run itself." Although we use this term in a general way, the men and women who designed the structure of prison envisioned a self-sustaining entity. This is where most of the jobs in prison originated. Plus, as we know very well, in life nothing is just black and white. There are always shades of grey. Those of us in prison know that it's the way they enforce these jobs that represents the dual purpose.

One of the first jobs that a person gets in prison is the field squad. While in the intake process, or waiting to see UCC the inmate.com grapevine is telling you, "Hey, if you go in there and tell them about the skills you got in a certain area, they will put you in that position. One of my homies got a job with the warden that way."

What's funny is that when you get into the interview with UCC they ask you, "Tell them about your work skills," as if they really plan to put you in the job that you want. If you don't have a medical restriction of some kind, then most likely your ass going to the fields. (smile).

This job was designed to provide fresh-grown produce for us to eat. It's cheaper if we grow our own food, but in the way they execute the job, you will think it's 1837 on a Mississippi plantation. Like we spoke about in earlier chapters, country boy rednecks ride upon horses with cowboy hats and loaded shotguns. They stare down upon you with contempt in their eyes and their words flow in cadence of aggression and demands that remind you of your current position in this world.

The weak fall victim to the mental and physical pressure. They allow their circumstance to define them instead of the other way around. The dual purpose of this job is thus revealed—it's meant to break your will, strip you of self-esteem and pride. Once this happens you have officially become an inmate/offender. Your mind is so fully engulfed with your current reality that you have redefined yourself in order to maintain a functional level of peace. You feel stuck, hopeless, and defeated internally, but the ego can't deal with the reality that you have redefined yourself in order to maintain a functional level of peace. The ego can't deal with the reality and heaviness of these emotions and so most just become one with the conditions they find themselves in.

In order to keep the inmate in his place, TDCJ places strict consequences on any violation of not showing up for work call. I've seen dudes who've laid it down go right to seg as an example of what happens to slaves who buck their position and new reality. You will know when someone has given into the new identity of their circumstance when they start to say things like, "It is what it is, bro" or they begin to seek positions within their jobs that can give them a sense of superiority. In the fields, this is the lead row or the tail row. This individual is usually appointed by the boss man and he is responsible for keeping the work flowing smooth. He does this by using "call and response" songs and rhythms to keep everyone in step and in-step with the flow. If someone is lagging, it's not uncommon for the lead row to say something to him to get him to get on pace with everyone else. In the old-time slavery, this person would be called the overseer. These positions allow one to keep intact the delicate balance of self-respect the ego needs in order to maintain tranquility.

We see this same mindset when it comes to dead end jobs out in society. For our purpose here we define a dead-end job as any job that stops your forward momentum, growth, and development, and drains your motivation to do better. Just like an inmate in prison, those stuck in the rat race feel they have no choice but to go to work. While an inmate, someone who has become one with the system, might get a case or go to seg for not going to work, someone out in society might not be able to pay bills or feed their kids. Most of the time, people are living lifestyles they can't afford which, in turn, makes them slaves to the jobs that help them maintain the image.

It's deeper than just consequence, those who are mentally and emotionally incarcerated with these jobs, with no key perspective (way of thinking that unlocks the limitations any circumstance tries to impose) are our focus here. These jobs are a part of a mindset, a belief in the limitations set upon one by generations before and by one's own doubts in how far one can go. Take this mindset and then add in the designed systematic strategies to keep certain people in place, the end result is someone stuck on the proverbial hamster wheel of life.

This person has made peace with the hamster wheel because, at their job, they are the supervisor. This position has become like a drug that numbs the mind to the internal unrest that whispers within.

In psychology, Freud called the ego's escape from reality "defense mechanisms," tactics that reduce or redirect anxiety by distorting reality. One of the biggest defense mechanisms that banishes from consciousness anxiety arousing thoughts, feelings, and memories, is denial.

In order to escape the reality of feeling stuck in these jobs, 45% of people stuck in these jobs feel they can't escape say they get high after work. Some take from works this helpless feeling and go home and dominate the home with an iron fist. In Freud's opinion, repression is incomplete, and it always comes out in another form, such as in dreams or slips of tongue. Other tactics the ego use are denial, displacement, rationalizations, and projection.

There is something different about the eyes of a lion in the cage at the zoo and a lion in the wild. Although the lion at the zoo eats every day, mates, and seems at peace, something is missing. It seems as though he lays around more than he explores, the fire in his eyes seems to have burned out. It's our belief that this same exploration spirit is missing in those stuck in the cages of their jobs. Yes, they eat daily, mate, and seem at peace, but in their minds, their conquering days are done. They tell themselves that it is too late, they are just too old or "next year is my year." Next year comes and it's still too late. They are a year older, and things just didn't work out the way they wanted this year, but next year they 'gone kill it.' The hamster wheel continues, and the owner of the hamster wheel sits back and enjoys the show.

Anais Nin once said that, "We don't see things as they are; we see things as we are." This truism holds water and power because we feel stuck in these circumstances not because we are actually trapped, but because we are stuck and trapped within the constraints of our minds. I once heard that a flea could jump and if you put it in a jar, it would try to jump out, hitting the lid of the jar every time. Then, with the lid of the jar removed, the flea would only jump as high as the lid was, not out of the jar.

Like the flea, we as people are so used to the limits in place that have stopped us over and over again in our lives, that we seem not to even notice when there is an opportunity to jump high into the freedom of our future. We jump into the next promotion at our current job instead of fighting for our dreams. In prison, we jump when our 'boss' asks us to do something and feel we have favor instead of becoming a full-time student to get that trade that will sustain us out in the world. Like Freud said, we use these things to "redirect anxiety by distorting reality." The most dangerous aspect of these mindsets is how Freud said they function, "all defense mechanisms function indirectly and unconsciously." When a common cold invades your body, you don't have to tell your blood cells to go to work fighting, the ego works the same way. It will automatically attempt to distort our reality if we don't remain 'dedicated to reality,' or having the ability to tell ourselves the truth no matter how painful and then take action to correct it.

These truths first poked their head out to me while I was working in the kitchen as a line server. I had moved my way from working on the floor wiping the tables off and filling the pitchers to serving on the line. The most coveted spot on the line is serving the main course. Eventually, I moved my way up to serving the main course and started making a lot of stamps (postage stamps are the common currency used to buy extra food). Nobody is going to give you a stamp for some extra green beans, but a piece of chicken is a different story.

When I first started out on the floor, I had dreams of becoming a cook and then one day working in the most coveted spot of all 'the ODR,' officer's dining area. Now that I was making 75-100 stamps a week, I told myself that cooks were slaves and the ODR was a place for dudes who had life sentences. Why would I leave when I was good?

In reality, I was fighting for crumbs. Working on the main you are expected to look out for your other coworkers who are serving the side dishes. The pot room workers expect you to leave them something to work with, and on top of that, line workers serve on the line then have to clean the line and the floor. Cooks were making a killing, and the dudes over in the ODR were maxin' & relaxin' fo' real: big screen TVs and access to free-world food on the regular.

I had opportunity after opportunity to move up and become a cook, but the lies I told myself had me stuck. Fate intervened when I got moved to the dorm. Out at P6 dorms, they had their own kitchen and I was reassigned to the kitchen out there. I asked to be put on the line serving the main, but my homeboy wasn't having it at all. He talked to the lady he knew, and she made me a diet-line cook. Instantly, my eyes were opened to how blind I had been! I couldn't believe the control and freedom I had as a cook versus a line worker; and the hustle, selling food, was crazy. I made so much commissary as a cook, I didn't have room in my locker to properly store it.

"Why had I been so blind?" "How could I have allowed myself to get so comfortable?" I realized that success had been my downfall. I had moved up from the floor and lost my vision. Then I had lied to myself to make it ok to stay stuck. Right then, I made up my mind that I would never allow success to stop me from moving forward and I would always remain dedicated to reality. An unknown wise woman once said a profound statement, "Our attitude towards life determines life's attitude towards us."

I changed my attitude and, let's just say, as of today, I work in the 'ODR' (smile). It's vital that we are diligent to being dedicated to reality in our lives. The things that come in and destroy our lives are but the small things that look harmless.

Let us take a moment to look at the story of Eve from The Bible. If we remember correctly from the story of the fall of man, we see that the Devil was more subtle than any beast of the field, he came in the form of a serpent. What we forget about this story is that Eve looked upon the apple as good. Good for food, pleasant to the eyes, and a tool to gain wisdom. She clearly knew what God had instructed them concerning the tree; she told the Devil, "God hath said, ye shall not eat of, neither shall ye touch it, lest ye die." So, my question to you is how does something we know will harm us become good in our minds?

The subtle things that get us play on our natural desires and thus we change our perspective in order to make them ok. Food and wisdom are things that we all desire. In the story of the fall of man, it didn't take much for the Devil to change Eve's perspective because he was using her own desires against her. We see this same dynamic in the gang life.

People don't join gangs to shoot other people, use drugs, and end up in prison! They join to fill their natural needs—love, acceptance, belonging. So, what I am saying is in our daily lives it is not drugs, alcohol, crime, and abuse that derail us, but subtle things like laziness, playing on the natural need for rest; complacency, playing on our natural need for security; and associations, playing on our need for human connection. This is how a 'good job' can really be the very thing that is keeping us from peace and our future potential. Also, why one must remain dedicated to reality.

My friend and coauthor, Buddy, learned this lesson from a life event that changed the course of this life. Buddy was 16-years old when he entered the rat race. A young man with ambition and a strong work ethic, he believed that hard work would get him to the top. Buddy was working at a grocery store as a bag boy. His job was to load the customers' items into bags and then assist them out to their car with a positive attitude.

On this particular day, Buddy was assisting an old-school gentleman with his bag and as they got closer to the cars, Buddy inched ahead towards the better of the two cars in the area.

Buddy said, "You in the Cadillac, right School?"

As School pulled his keys out, he shook his head and said, "No, youngster, I'm in the old Camry."

Maybe it was a look that School seen in Buddy's eyes, or just School feeling like sharing a bit of wisdom to a youngster who reminded him of himself, School opened up.

"Youngster, I had big dreams and ambitions when I was your age. I look around at my life now and I sometimes wonder how things turned out so beneath my potential. I think maybe I shouldn't have listened to people when it came to my ideas and dreams. My past failures also played a big part in what I believed I could achieve. At the end of the day, this is my life. It is what it is, youngster. Whatever you do just keep believing."

Buddy nodded his head, not really knowing what to say. He helped school load his bags into his car and stood there as he drove off. For the rest of the day, Old-School's words echoed in Buddy's mind and heart. "I shouldn't have listened to people when it came to my ideas and dreams… my past failures played a big part in what I believed I could achieve… keep believing…"

During his daily break that same day, Buddy was looking through Facebook and came across a post that said, "Knowledge speaks, but wisdom listens." –Jimmy Hendrix. Buddy thought about the people he'd came across whom had great ideas and theories but very few acted upon them. Right then, he made a decision that we would never end up like School. If he was going to work hard, it would be for himself. Forget what everyone around him was saying about what and how he should be living his life. He decided to listen to his heart and 'go get it.!' Six months later, he was driving a brand-new Infiniti G37 and not looking back.

Looking back, we can see that Buddy had the right mindset with the wrong idea connected to it, but that hunger to never settle for less, and to go hard at all cost, lead to this transformation here in prison.

When I think about School and those people who end up under a bridge somewhere in a crowded city begging for change, the question 'how,' always pops in my mind. How could someone give up on their dreams to the point that they become like the walking dead? Waking up every day just going through the motions, no real vision, no passion, no risks, just surviving. Maybe the answer lies in what School said, maybe we start to doubt our true potential and we give in to what the people around us tell us is possible. Like Eve, we believe that giving in to what looks good won't really kill us. After all, how many people don't' even have jobs? Finally, we bite into the rat race apple and the bottom falls out from under our dreams and we wake up one day and realize that our passion did die, our determination did die, our vision did die, and we are now the walking dead.

Another question comes to mind when I think about School from Buddy's story and people whom end up living under a bridge, or just people in general who have given up on their vision—How do I not end up like that?

How do we not allow doubts, fears, and challenges to railroad us to the point of losing traction? Through soul-searching and waking up daily with intent and focus, we have found the answer and the keys that can set you free in this area of your life.

We started this chapter off talking about the first job that most people get starting off in prison, the field squad. When we used the word 'inmate,' it was in reference to a prisoner who has become one with the system, instead of being focused on the direction of his life and how he would structure his time, his time has structured him. This same dynamic happens to those who become stuck in the rat race, they have given up on their personal dreams and have accepted the status quo as reality, with no escape.

The first step to getting out of the fields in prison and escaping the rat race is vision. Vision is knowing where you are headed in life, it's your mental picture and roadmap that guides your decisions. Buddy spoke about vision and encouraged that it would keep you on track when everything around you looked dark. It's simply your map. With this inner map, it doesn't matter where you start, and a wrong turn is really no cause for concern because you know where the end destination is and how to get back on track from where you are. Just like a real map tells you your next turn, your inner maps tells you your next step to get closer to your destination. Without this map, or vision, one can get lost and end up calling a place home that's not the destination.

Next, we must admit that we all have to start somewhere. We talked about this aspect in the very first chapter called 'Intake.' In this starting place, it is vital that you start maximizing the learning opportunities and making network connections that complement the vision you have for your future. As a cook in the kitchen here in prison, I had my eye getting into the ODR, but while I was a cook, I maxed the position out for all that it was worth. First, I applied for an on-the-job training (OJT) certificate, so that one day, parole can see that I was learning even while I was at work. I hustled to the max and found out a way to turn the stamps that I made from food I sold into money on my books. My locker is full, and my books are sitting fat. Last, but not least, I made sure I knew who all the ODR workers were and made connections with them in various ways. Maximize where you are! If you have a dream of running your own company, why not start learning the ebb and flow of a company right where you are? When the boss walks in, watch how he carries himself. When he speaks at meetings, take notes on what you like about his style and things you would do different. Start networking with like-minded individuals whom you can bounce ideas off of and maybe start partnerships with but be careful whom you share your dreams with.

This advice leads right into our next step, while you are maximizing where you are, make sure that you keep your eyes on your vision and that you are taking concrete steps daily in the direction of your dreams. Maybe this means saving money, working on a business plan daily for thirty minutes, or just surfing the internet for relevant info that pertains to your future goals. They say Rome wasn't built in a day and trust us, your dreams wont' either. Plant daily seeds that will help you keep your eyes on the prize.

Last, but not least my friends, you must realize that all seeds that are planted go through a gestation period. Before you actually see the plant above ground it is already developing and getting ready to break through the dirt. This same principle applies to your dreams; determination will be mostly unseen. But, when you sprout my friend, the fruit of your work will feed you and maybe many generations that come after you!

Many people are sitting around waiting on things to change. They're waiting for the easy way to present itself. They looking to piggyback on the back of those with ambition, grit, and focused determination. They even pray to a God who has given them the world, the laws of sowing and reaping, and their mind, body, and spirit expecting him to do more. I tell you my friend, they are in for a long wait. Anon said it best, "Things may come to those who wait, but only the things left by those who hustle."

Your dreams are not going to come to you, you got to go get it!

KEYS TO FREEDOM

The average retirement age in America is sixty-five years old. Many people have to work years past their golden years to still be able to afford the basic cost of living. With taking out such a large chunk of our lives, it would be wise to do something we love and care about. But, as in most things in life, this isn't' always the case.

The work we do in our early lives is usually an entry-level position.

It starts off as a basic job to take care of our young selves, but it turns out to be a life-long trap due to life's unexpected events and human nature—conformity, complacency, laziness, etc. How we view ourselves determines our trajectory in work and life. In order to avoid these traps in life, we must learn to use the humble beginnings as steppingstones and not security blankets.

Seeing yourself destined for greatness is crucial, but the work that we have to put into our life goals are just as important. As you work for others, work for yourself, use these steppingstones as a life-long educational process toward what you want out of life. This is how you maximize work call.

YEAR #7: CASES

—————⟨⟩o⟨⟩⟨⟩o⟨⟩—————

G ive me your ID!" When you hear this statement in prison, nine times out of ten, you are about to get a 'case.' In simple terms, the definition of a case is a written and recorded violation against you for violating TDCJ policy. When a corrections officer (CO) asks for your identification card, it's so that they can write down your name and TDCJ number, for a number of different reasons. Based on how the case is graded is what determines the seriousness of the punishment. You can get a case that is determined a minor violation all the way up to what is called a major violation.

Minor violations include things such as disobeying a direct order, talking while in commissary line, or trafficking and trading (moving commissary from one wing/dorm to another or just trading items with another person, such as food on your tray). Major cases here in prison include things such as fighting, possession of contraband such as weed or tobacco, or an assault on an officer.

After the case is written, a disciplinary hearing will be arranged to determine whether you are guilty or not. If you are found guilty, which in 90% of cases you will be, then most times you will receive your punishment on the spot. Punishment for minor cases most commonly include things like 15 days commissary restriction, this means that from the day of your hearing you will have to wait 15 days before you can go back to the commissary. Rec restrictions are also another common punishment for minor cases. If you get, say, 30 days rec restriction, then for the next month when they call rec, you must stay on the wing.

In reality, based on what unit you are on will determine what rules are truly enforced. This dynamic is played out when it comes down to each particular officer also. On Hightower unit in Dayton, Texas, if you look back at a woman guard who is passing by as you stand in the commissary line, you will most likely get a case and get kicked out of the line. On Coffield, the commissary line is damn near like the 'ho stroll,' dudes looking back, whistling, and everything in between. Each unit has its own culture, but the general observation seems to follow the logic that if the unit is known for drugs, fights, and gangs, then they really don't' sweat the small stuff as much.

If the unit is a fairly slow unit that isn't gang and drug infested, than a haircut with a fade is a major thing. How else will they pass time and feel superior at the same time, all in the name of change (smile).

First, it's your responsibility to know the culture of the unit, and then through questions and observation, know which officers enforce which rules. In the book called Mastery, Robert Greene would call this initial phase the "apprenticeship phase." This phase is all about observation and knowledge. This is where you learn the ebb and flow of the system, you watching other people 'cluck out' or 'crash,' get in trouble on some fluke or dumb shit, and you taking mental notes of how to do your time and not allow it to do you.

This wisdom and observation, even when mastered, will not keep you from occasionally getting a case. GETTING CASES IS INEVITABLE! They are a part of doing time. Inmate.com even says that if you see parole without a case on your record, they will say that 'you manipulated the system.' We have a whole chapter on believing what Inmate.com says, but one thing I can say is that I agree with Robert Greene. In his book *The 48 Laws of Power*, he says to not ever "appear to be perfect." This imperfection somehow makes one seem more human. So, when it comes to seeing parole, cases show that you are growing and getting better if you don't have too many.

There is a key component that we want to highlight when it comes to these cases that we get as part of doing time. This dynamic will make the difference between how productive you are moving forward after we make bad choices and decisions or get cases. This dynamic is accepting responsibility. The opposite of this quality is, of course, denying responsibility and this is what you would see from most men in prison if you could sit in on a disciplinary hearing or when they have to give an initial statement on what happened when they got the case.

Officer: "So, what is your statement?"

Man in prison: "So, look, Sarge, man that officer got something against me. I think he prejudice. I came back from school and they tell me I got a e.comm [food purchased by family and distributed from commissary window] and so I go to the window to get my stuff. When he see me in line, he say I'm 'out of place' and to give him my ID. How am I out of place when I got a e.comm that my family done paid fo?"

Officer: "When you say 'they' said you had an e.comm, who is 'they?'"

Man in prison: "My homeboys, they told me as soon as I came in from school."

Officer: "Can your homeboys give you permission to go anywhere or are you supposed to check in with one of my officers and get a pass?"

Man in prison: "It ain't my fault they said I got an e.comm! So, you just gone ride with that prejudice ass lawman, I ain't trippin', do what you gotta do!"

This individual has not mastered the skill of accepting responsibility. Instead, everything that happens to him is a result of something or someone else whom is against him. It's never his fault, blame is his weapon and denial is the defense mechanism his ego uses to shake anxiety.

If he had mastered this vital life skill, this man in prison would have put himself in a favorable position to maybe get out of the case, but at the very least own his choices and accepting he is in control of his life and the results that follow.

Officer: "So what is your statement?"

Man in prison: "First off, I see where my mistake was, sir. When my friends told me I had an e.comm, I should have stopped and gotten a pass, but I allowed my excitement to get the best of me and went to the commissary window when they called chow, that's on me. If you would look at my record, you will see that I'm no troublemaker and hardly ever get cases. It's my hope that you would take into consideration and decide to solve this issue informally. It won't happen again."

I call this dynamic the Law of Forgiveness. This law has its foundation in the spiritual realm, but we see it's evidence in nature when it comes to medicine. For most ailments there is a natural cure with the exact components that will restore its health. When it comes to mental and emotional wounds and offenses, the natural cure are sometimes words of mercy and repentance. These words when applied to an offence bring back healing and internal peace. So, when we enter a situation in where there has been an offense, when you ask forgiveness, we bring natural laws of understanding and mercy into our favor.

Even if there must be a consequence for the offense, the person who applies the law of forgiveness guards his heart from bitterness that comes from feeling that the results of your life are not out of your control. In essence, you forgive yourself and protect yourself from stagnation of blame.

Out in society, a case can be brought against you for anything from a speeding ticket, theft, all the way up to murder. The consequences as we know can range from losing your license, a couple of months in the county jail, all the way to life in prison.

I remember reading a quote by Sigmund Freud that said, "People want freedom, but freedom involves responsibility, and most people are frightened of responsibilities."

When I think about how freedom and responsibility go hand in hand, I think about the conversations that I have with my son on the nature of what a real man is. I do my best to make sure he understands that an individual's age doesn't make them a man. In order to enter the freedom that manhood offers, one must master responsibility. I tell my son that the moment that he can successfully be responsible for the vision he has constructed for his life and execute that vision with wisdom, common sense, and hard work, then he will own the freedom that goes hand in hand with manhood.

On the other side of this same coin, Freud spoke of those whom "fear this responsibility." In essence, we could say that they fear freedom. Scott Peck learned from the author Erich Fromm and his study of Nazism and authoritarianism that this dynamic is called, "Escape from freedom." In his book, *The Road Less Traveled*, Peck tells a story of his spending more time with patients than other colleagues and how this choice had led him to resentment. He goes to his supervisor and attempts to get some help. After explaining his dilemma, over and over his supervisor would respond with, "I see that you do have a problem."

Finally, Peck exploded, "God dammit, I know I have a problem. I knew that when I came in here. The question is, what am I going to do about it?"

His supervisor again responded, "Scott, I want you to listen. Listen closely and I will say it again. I agree with you. You do have a problem. Specifically, you have a problem with your time. Your time. Not my time, it's not my problem. It's your problem with your time. You, Scott Peck, have problems with your time. That's all I'm going to say about it."

Peck stormed out of the office and it took him a couple months to come to terms with the lessons. He was attempting to escape from the freedom of how he spent his time by trying to give his supervisor his power. He said, "By requesting Mac Badgely to assume responsibility for the structure of my time, I was attempting to avoid the pain of working long hours, even though working long hours was inevitable consequence of my choice."

In close conjunction with our freedom out there in society is the skill of being able to accept responsibility for our choices. Especially when it comes to the cases that are brought against us. When we attempt to avoid the pain of our choices, we stay stuck in a cycle of blame, our life in our minds are not our own, but the result of the things that happen to us. If we believe this way our ego can be saved the pain. In exchange for this safety, we get charged a hefty fee—we remain mentally and emotionally incarcerated, bound by fear when in reality, fear is false evidence appearing real.

Out in society I used to blame the white man for the choices and decisions that I had to make to survive. As long as the results of my life were the results of a corrupted system, I felt justified in the laws I broke in order to make it. While reading one day, I happened upon a quote by William Burrough that said, "A man can fail many times, but he isn't a failure until he begins to blame someone else." This truism hit me like a ton of bricks. My whole life I had been blaming others for my actions and choices. No! I had different options. Accepting this truth gave me such a feeling of power and control over my life. No longer was I a black man controlled by the conditions of my life. Instead of escaping from freedom, I escaped the pen that held me captive for so long.

This lesson cost Buddy $8 to learn when he was at his second transfer unit. At the Lopez Unit, Buddy was still green and learning the ropes of TDCJ. At commissary he had just recently bought a white shirt that cost $8 (yeah, they killin' the game). One day after washing his shirt, Buddy was looking around for a place to hang/dry his shirt and so he just decided to hang it off of the edge of his bunk.

An officer came into the dorm in order to do his rounds and noticed Buddy's shirt hanging from the edge of his bed.

He grabbed the shirt, "whose shirt is this?"

Buddy said, "Oh, that's me sir, I was letting it dry."

"You're not supposed to hang anything from your bunk, its posted in the rule book," the officer said.

"Oh, my bad, sir. I didn't know," Buddy said.

"Well, 'I didn't know,' ain't gone cut it for me when I get pulled over in the world, and it ain't' about to work for you now. Let me see your ID."

Whenever you get a case a Sergeant is assigned to take your statement before you have the actual hearing. The Sarge has the power to throw the case out if he believes that it can be solved informally. Buddy walked in and the Sarge asked him his statement.

Buddy said, "Sarge, I really didn't know I couldn't hang my shirt off my bed, but that's on me because I should have read in the handbook or at least asked around the dorm. I'm new at this unit and I be staying out the way. If you let me make it, you won't have no trouble no more."

"I like the way you didn't' come in here with no attitude like most. Plus, you owned up to your shit like a man, I done had dudes come in here plea bargaining and snitching over less. Look, I'm taking the shirt, but I'm ripping the case up. I don't want to see you in front of me again," the Sargent said.

"That's cool," Buddy said as he got up and walked out of the office.

Nelson Bowell said, "The difference between greatness and mediocracy is often in how an individual views a mistake."

When one views a mistake from the lens of his choices, the power of change is possible. If the lens is pointed in the direction of another, then unconsciously we remain powerless and stuck within the prisons that enslave us. In order for us to solve the issues that take us captive, we must first look within and acknowledge the power we have to choose to change. This starts with accepting responsibility.

If you have really been paying attention for a common theme throughout our writing, you will find that choices are the foundation a lot of these principles stand on.

Thank God this lesson only cost Buddy $8 (smile).

So far, we have discussed how the skill of accepting responsibility serves us in two ways. On one side of the coin, it activates the law of forgiveness in some cases, and allows us to receive the medicine of mercy and grace for our transgressions. On the other side, it serves as a gateway into man/womanhood helping us to maintain the freedom to choose in every circumstance that we face in life. We also touched on the fact that when we have the fortitude to accept responsibility for our actions it fosters in us an awareness that we are in control of our lives and not the other way around. This is called an internal locus of control.

There is an aspect about cases both in and out of prison that I want to touch on before we close the chapter.

Behind every case is a law or rule that predicates it. We have all heard the saying that 'rules are created to be broken.' In reality, this mentality is reckless because most laws were created with order and protection in mind. The world we live in would look something like the movie *Mad Max* or *The Book of Eli* if cases weren't motivation to follow the laws of the land. Anarchy would be the end result and every man for himself would be the creed of the day. I wonder sometimes what it is in men/woman that needs the fear of consequences to prevent them from taking another person's property, violating another's body, or even taking one's life. Some believe that self-preservation leads the way when it comes to natural instincts that lead to justification for crime. Whatever we end up calling this dark side of human nature, it's evident that laws and cases are needed to shape behavior.

From the psychology perspective 'shaping' is an operant conditioning procedure in which reinforcers guide behavior toward closer approximation of the desired behavior. In prison, the reinforcers are the guards, and cases are tools they use to guide behavior closer to what they desire. In society, laws guide behavior and police, in this instance, would be the reinforcers. Let's take a look at some of the reasons why we feel that cases are an intricate part of our society. In 2017, 10,874 motor vehicle traffic deaths involved someone who was behind the wheel drunk. Each year, it seems as though this number continues to climb. Imagine the number of alcohol related deaths in our nation if there weren't any case/laws against DWI.

In this perspective, we can start to see and understand that laws, and cases that come from violating these laws, aren't meant to restrict us but actually to protect our lives and others.

Also, in the year 2017, over 70,200 people overdosed on a variety of drugs such as heroin, cocaine, anti-depressants, and prescription opioids. 70,000! In recent years, there has been a massive crackdown by the reinforcers on pharmacies and even doctors for over-prescribing drugs. Without these cases, the number of deaths when it comes to these drugs would be astronomical. Sometimes the threat of cases saves us from ourselves.

Right now, as we speak, there is a massive fight going on between gun lobbyists and the National Rifle Association (NRA). Between 2016 and 2019, there have been over 319 mass shootings! With the threat of new cases for owning guns that are automatic or hold more than a certain number of rounds, the reinforcers are attempting to shape behavior and save lives.

There is a quote by Mabel Collins that says, "Each man is his own absolute law giver, the dispenser of glory or gloom to himself; the decreer of his life, his reward, his punishment."

Even though we have laws that are designed to protect and keep order, this quote says that each man/woman is to accept and acknowledge the fact each day you are responsible for your choices and actions. The consequences for your actions will mirror the laws of cause and effect and thus bring back to you what you choose. Whether rewards or punishment, gloom or glory, your life is a reflection not of the cases that effect you, but the laws that you have given yourself.

KEYS TO FREEDOM

When you're trying to go home, the last thing you want is a case on your record. Nobody wants them, but everybody at some point of their sentence will receive one. The feelings most have when getting a case is often accompanied by fear, regret, and anger, because you won't know the punishment until the case is served to you.

In some instances, ignorance plays a part of it, but in others, it's just plain old "bucking," disobeying the law, because most of the laws are unreasonable. Like the one instance I needed to hang dry my new t-shirt while it was still warm in the daytime. Rather than trying to hang dry it at night, TDCJ policy states that we can only hang dry our clothes from 6 pm -6 am, but that's just the reality in prison where up is down and down is up.

The purpose of life is being able to recognize those moments where the laws, rules, and cases are not things that we must simply obey, but things that we must fight to change. Laws that go against equality, justice, and freedom—universal laws.

Here in prison, there will often be times where people will go hungry due to the fact prison only supplies a person enough to sustain themselves, regardless of how many calories they've burned working for the system. So, if I wanted to help someone in need with some food I purchase off commissary, I would be in violation of rule 3, traffic, and trading. Or, if I witness someone being jumped by gang members for no reason other than sitting on a gang bench and decided to help, I would be punished for being in a riot, but morally and ethically correct.

Historically, had it not been for the civil right fighters of the past, like Martin Luther King, Jr., Rosa Parks, and those that fought before them, life in America would not be as it is today. The boycotts and sit-ins of the 1960s helped change the laws of the day and got many Americans thinking about racism in a new light.

Although cases were designed to control behavior, how we use them leads us to freedom. When it comes to the cases in your life, accepting responsibility so that mentally you don't become a slave to life and things happening to you. Also, use wisdom when it comes to what you allow to control your behavior. Be a slave to nothing! This is the key!

YEAR #8: GRIEVANCE

In some circles when someone has a conflict with another, you might hear them say, "I got a grievance with you!" In other's the approach is more direct, "Why the fu** did you…?" In any case, if you were to look up the definition of a 'grievance' in Webster's Dictionary, it would say it was "an actual or supposed circumstance regarded as just cause for complaint." They had no choice but to add the word "supposed" to their definition because no matter if the situation was actual, my perception of the circumstance is all it takes for a conflict to ensue.

In TDCJ, a grievance is a form used to file a complaint. These forms can be found or obtained most times by just asking an officer. If you're having conflict with an officer and you say, "Give me a grievance," nine times out of ten he/she will make the process difficult, but they still can't refuse you this form. If the officer is stalling you out and taking his/her time in giving you one then you can get a grievance form from the law library, housing areas, shift supervisors, or by putting in an I-60 request form and this method will get you a grievance form within a few days.

So, what can I file a grievance on? Knowing what is grievable is knowledge that is useful and will help you in not wasting one of your most valuable assets, time. One can file a grievance on a number of things. Let's say, for example, that my living area is shook down or searched by an officer, and the officer damages my family pictures or any of my personal property, then I have the right to file a grievance on that officer. If I have an issue with a particular officer and I go to his/her supervisor with my issue and then this same officer starts harassing me by searching my cell every time he/she works, or strip searching me just because, then I can file a grievance on this officer citing the offense of retaliation. Another grievable issue are the conditions of the prison. The extreme heat in the summer has been an ongoing fight through the grievance system and even the courts. Small victories have been won when it comes to the religious rights through the grievance process. We can now wear religious beards based on these victories.

You would just be wasting your time if you wrote a grievance saying, "I just got denied parole and I swear I'm a changed man." You just might get the form back with a big LOL on it. Even if you had a valid reason, but took too long to write the grievance, "I'm writing Mr. Smith up for slapping me real hard three years ago, "you still might get a chuckle out of the grievance officer.

For all purposes and intents, filing a grievance is about conflict resolution, this is in prison and out in the free world. Just like when it comes to the grievance process, you have to understand so that you can use the system effectively, solving our issues when it comes to personal conflicts takes understating certain skills. Just like some issues in prison are not grievable, one must know which issues are even worth fighting over. My grandfather used to call this skill "Knowing how to choose your battles." We have all met the drama king/queen who seems to have an issue with something all the time and don't have a problem letting you know. On the other end of the spectrum, we have those who won't say anything out of fear of conflict; they feel like their issues in their marriage will just solve themselves. They believe that with age, they will just naturally become wiser without digging deep into the dark places that hold them hostage and stuck in certain behaviors. Then you have the balanced individual who seems to understand that solving problems is a part of this life we live and attempting to avoid them will, in return, breed more.

My boy, Scott Peck, spoke on this issue and said, "To willingly confront a problem early, before we are forced to confront it by circumstances, means to put aside something pleasant or less painful for something more painful. It is choosing to suffer now in hope of the future gratification rather than choosing to continue present gratification in hope that future suffering will not be necessary."

This is the mindset that we must adopt if we wish to transcend the conflicts that arise in our lives. This thinking is powerful because it is not achieved by the ease and comfort of pleasantries that attempt to cover potential issues. It stays vigilant and on alert for issues that present a potential threat to future success. Once an issue is identified, it is addressed.

To tell the whole truth and nothing but the truth, most dudes in prison don't even write grievances, even when they have valid reasons. Inmate.com has led them to believe that it is utterly useless to write a grievance because officers are only going to look out for their own when it comes to a choice between them and us. These individuals just deal with injustice the best way they know how or just 'charge it to the game,' or take a loss.

It's not a rare occurrence to see this mindset flow over into their personal lives when it comes to problems solving and relational issues. Either they delay addressing issues until it's too late or they avoid the reality of the issue altogether.

Then we find what in prison is called a 'writ writer.' And those like them who understand the power of standing up for your rights and addressing issues head-on, whether win or lose. My pops used to tell me all the time, "Son, if I lose a fight, I promise my opponent will never mess with me again. Sometimes a win cost too much."

In this I came to understand that when you have the courage to face your issues, when you have the self-respect to stand up for what is right, even if you lose, you still win respect. Not only yourself, but from those that feel like they can test your resolve. Conflict resolution is not about fighting with your fists, our purpose here, and throughout our book, is to show you that the most powerful weapon that you have is your mind. Writ writers and those alike go to the law library and study the PD-22, Officer's Conduct Handbook and Rules. They learn the proper codes and when they file grievances, they put these codes on the form and speak their language. When they encounter these officers again, you can tell by the look in their eyes and their tone of voice that a new level of respect has been obtained.

Fighting with our minds to solve our relational issues with one another should also be the same. Eye to eye contact, tone of voice, listening, solution focus, and having an overall understanding of the individual that we are dealing with shows a sharpened mind in the area of conflict resolution. Eric Hoffer said it this way, "You can discover what your enemy fears most by observing the means he uses to frighten you."

In these encounters, resolution should be the focal point so even when we are dealing with an attack, through calm patience and listening, we will be able to use tact to solve the issue. When we inflame the situation with our own attitude or avoid it by hanging up the phone or walking away, resolution is hardly ever achieved. We are not saying that walking away from a situation or a relationship is never the answer but should come after other options have been exhausted.

Learning to resolve your issues and problems is a source of tremendous growth. The pain and discomfort that we experience from these issues cause us to dig deep within our minds and souls for answers. This digging allows us to uncover the treasures of our strength. This in turn adds wisdom and understanding to our daily lives and as we walk in this consciousness, we are protected from getting in the way of our blessings. Just think, one second of anger can cost you a lifetime of trouble.

In the wild jungles of Africa, they say that a lioness will follow a pregnant gazelle and her herd for up to three days. Never does she give chase, she has mastered the telltale signs of a pregnant gazelle and she knows that when the gazelle drops and goes into labor pains there will be nothing it can do. Right before we give birth to our greatest blessings, we will receive some of our greatest attacks! This is a vital lesson that we should never lose sight of when it comes to how we choose to solve our conflicts. Like the lioness, our problems follow and attack us when we least expect them to, if they are not met head on and solved. I guess the male gazelle assumed that by ignoring the lioness, she will just somehow disappear. :)

One of the greatest misconceptions of our time is people feeling that their issues, problems, and conflicts will somehow just go away. No matter how much weed you smoke, cocaine you snort, or alcohol you drink, when the high is gone, the problems remain. Aldous Huxley once said, "In the course of history many more people have died for their drink or their dope than have died for their religion or their country." If I was a betting man, I'd put it all on my belief that at least half of these people were attempting to avoid some type of problem or pain.

It's only when we face these grievances head on that we find the keys to freedom that lie within the darkness of our pains.

One of the grimmest realities of avoiding the grievances that we face in life is the reality of suicide. To imagine that a problem can seem so insurmountable in one's mind is surreal.

I worked in the same kitchen 3 ½ years ago, back in seg. They are not allowed to leave their cells for the most part and so we have a makeshift kitchen down on the seg cellblock where we make their trays and deliver it to them in their cell. We make the trays and then the Service Support Inmate (SSI) takes the food up to each cell. One day, one of the SSIs came to me with a message.

"Say B.O.B., this dude upstairs on J-wing say he think he your kinfolk. He say him and your bro Clue use to kick it real tuff. When you get some time, go up there and holla at him," the SSI said.

"Let him know that I'll slide through. If he know my lil bro, then he definitely know ya boy," I said.

Before I went up on J-wing, I did my homework. Sometimes this is a set-up. You get on the wing and walk up to a cell front and get speared in the eye with a makeshift spear. Or, you get dashed in the face with a cupful of piss or semen. After everything panned out, I made my way over to J-wing and pulled up on my kinfolk.

His cell front was covered by a thick blanket and so I spoke through it, "Say bro, you sent me a message to come holla at you."

Nothing happened, no response, "You in there bro," I said.

Finally, I saw a light come on and he pulled the blanket to the side. It was hard to see his face. "What's good Lil-cuzz? It's been a long-time kinfolk," he said.

I looked closer. "Lil-Ronnie," I said, "Damn you look different."

From the look in his eyes, I could tell that he was alive but not living. The struggles of life were all over his face, but for the moment he had a smile on his face. For the next twenty minutes, we talked about life, love, the hood, family, and doing time. He made sure to tell me that if I ever needed anything, not to hesitate to ask. I, in turn, let him know that I would be sending him extra food on his tray from that day forward.

Over the next month or so we looked out for one another and when it was good, I would drop by every so often to make sure he was good. One night, while I was at work at my new job in the ODR, an officer came in and asked me did I know the dude on J-wing who had hung himself. I told him no and thought nothing more of it. When I got back on the dorm, my boy Slim informed me that he had a kite or note for me from a SSI in seg. In the kite it told me that my kinfolk, Ronald Lee Jones, had hung himself and committed suicide! I sat on the edge of my bunk in disbelief. I thought back to the pain I used to see in his eyes and questioned how I had allowed his smile to distract me. I instantly asked myself if there was more I could have said, done, etc. I didn't blame myself, but I vowed that I would make sure to never be fooled by smiles again. I would at least ask if I could maybe be an ear for whatever someone might be dealing with. Instead of just shooting the shit, or having a shallow conversation, I should have been asking what I could have done to help with the grievances of his heart. This failure of mine motivated me to be that much better of a life coach; never again would I allow pain to hide from me. How life lessons from the pen can set you free.

We may never understand the gravity of what my kinfolk was dealing with, but through the gruesome act of suicide, we can see the importance of having the skills to solve our problems. We can learn the consequences of avoiding or thinking they will just go away. They must be faced. Rest in Power, Ronald Lee Jones.

Buddy learned the power of facing problems head-on from several different situations throughout his life, but one in particular occurred while he was doing time at the Hightower unit.

At this time of his life, Buddy was 26 years old and he was ambitiously attempting to earn his GED in Mr. Foster's class. Buddy understood that education was the key to unlocking the potential his future contained and nothing could deter him from his goal of obtaining his GED.

Buddy was always at Mr. Foster's desk asking questions to gain a deeper understanding in areas where he struggled. Mr. Foster appreciated Buddy's hunger for learning and took a liking to him making it his mission to help Buddy reach his goal.

But on the path to success, there are always obstacles, and this time they came in the form of a lady named Ms. Craven. She came up with the idea in her head that Mr. Foster was showing Buddy favoritism and she tried to write him up for establishing a relationship, which is a major case.

The next day when Buddy attempted to enter the school at the check-in desk, he was told by the officer he was no longer on the roster. Buddy dropped his head in disbelief, left the schoolhouse and grabbed a step 1 grievance before he even made it back on the wing. Nothing was going to get in his way, he had come too far to allow the darkness within Ms. Craven to stop his progress. He had survived the streets, he had beat death, and had conquered himself; Craven was no match for his strength within.

After filing his step 1 grievance, Buddy put in an I-60 to have an interview with the principal and even wrote a letter to the warden. See, Buddy knew that without a fight, without standing up for what you believed in, without fighting for your rights and facing the challenges that attempt to derail you, this world will swallow you whole and then spit you out. He knew that this problem wouldn't just solve itself and go away. He also understood that inaction was one of the highest forms of action and he looked the issue in the eye.

After a week, they still hadn't called him to serve him the case for establishing a relationship. He found out that Ms. Craven couldn't write the case because she had so little evidence to back up her bogus claims. He wondered, if this was the case, how the hell had they kicked him out of school? He wrote to the principal again. Twenty-six days after it all began, Buddy was called to the principal's office for a meeting. As Buddy sat looking the principal in her eyes, she explained how unfortunate the situation was but how she had to take her officer's word seriously. She explained that she at least had to investigate the issue and after doing so, she said that Ms. Craven had a history of making these claims against students whom Mr. Foster saw potential in, and that the matter was being looked into deeper.

The principal explained to Buddy that some of the other students that Ms. Craven had made this claim against had never returned to finish school. Because of Buddy's fight, the spotlight was now on Ms. Craven and her motives.

Buddy was immediately assigned to another teacher's class to finish his GED, he passed with the top grade in his class on the first try! As Buddy stoop proud at his graduation, he looked out into the crowd and saw not only the principle clapping but Ms. Craven!

Later on down the road, in a turn of events, Buddy was called down to school again, this time for an interview with Ms. Craven, herself. As Buddy sat across from her, he could tell something was different about the way she felt about him when it came to respect. She apologized in her own way for what she said she felt she had to do. Nevertheless, she mentioned how she admired Buddy's fight, his determination, and his dedication to his vision, and she needed someone like him working in the school.

Maybe some of how she felt was true, but Buddy sensed that the pressure from Huntsville, the principal, and the letters he had written was playing a major part on her attempting to make amends. After she was finished talking, he thanked her but politely declined the job, stood up and walked off. Never again did he have an issue with Ms. Craven, and some of the dudes who were kicked out in the past by accusations made by Ms. Craven were motivated by Buddy's fight to see what could be done in their case.

Malcom X said, "Usually when people are sad, they don't do anything, they just cry over their condition. But when angry, they bring about change."

Whatever our grievance may be, if we would look upon them as obstacles trying to steal our passion, our peace, our dreams, then we would become angry at them and fight for the changes that will allow us to use our issues as stepping stones.

One key aspect about the grievance process here in prison is the fact that before you write the grievance you must attempt to informally resolve the problem. This means that before I write a grievance on an officer for retaliating against me, I must either speak to that officer or speak to his/her supervisor and allow them to attempt to help me. In our lives, the grievance would then represent the last resort, and us attempting to formally resolve our issues would represent our fight to solve our issues before we ever reach that point.

In our marriages, this could mean counseling before divorce. In our jobs, this might be talking to the supervisor before we actually file a written complaint. Here in prison, this could mean having a man-to-man before we go to that blind spot to fight.

Our problems result from the fact that we sometimes feel that our problems will somehow just disappear—we smoke cigarettes, drink, and do drugs believing that they're somehow helping when in reality, these behaviors are adding to our issues.

When it comes to the grievances that we have with one another we lack the skills to find the root of the issue and so we stay on surface issues that drain our energy and waste valuable time we can never get back. Just like writ writers had to develop the knowledge and wisdom to effectively solve their issues in a way that bring results, we too, must equip ourselves with conflict resolution skills on a diverse scale. We must, in order to navigate this life, know how to solve both internal and external grievances that plague us throughout life. Without these skills, we at times feel so drained and burdened that the weight is just too much, and we want to end it all!

We wish that we could tell you exactly what to do to solve each issue you face. That would be a multimillion-dollar book in itself (smile). Whatever the solution, our purpose here is to make sure that you understand that your grievances MUST BE FACED! They will not just go away. Conflict resolution is a mindset of will and determination and Mrs. Angela Davis said something profound about this when she said, "I am no longer accepting the things I cannot change, I'm changing the things I cannot accept."

This mental attitude is the key to conflict resolution. Buddy changed a situation that he could not accept while the others before him just accepted what they felt they were powerless to change. When we face our grievances and overcome, we build within us a strength and confidence that sustains us through the storms of life. For us who have this mindset, facing our challenges becomes almost like a habit and the energy that we release, based on the laws of attraction, somehow even starts to limit life's attempts at distracting us! You know you square business when life itself stay out of your way (smile).

KEYS TO FREEDOM

A lot of the battles we face in life are not physical, they're political. The grievance process in prison is similar to a lawsuit being sought by a plaintiff against a defendant. In a court setting, each side has an objective—to come out as a victor. In prison, as stated earlier in this chapter, this is one of the few ways we have to get justice, but it is often to no avail because, as in most matters in prison, we are often presumed guilty by the fact that we are still incarcerated.

Politics is itself a language, an art form. The whole world witnessed the 2020 Presidential elections where Joe Biden defeated Donald Trump by a wide margin. Donald Trump has, and still continues to, file lawsuits in order to reverse the results of the elections, which are all political moves to disrupt the transitional phase of the president-elect, Joe Biden. Still, the mass majority of Trump supporters who don't understand politics get caught up in the political fog and can't see the political game for what it is.

Grievances/complaints are effects of political moves that are made between humans that are caused when a party issues a suit against a defendant. Whether these suits are based on truth or lies isn't the case, it's having the ability to recognize when these political attacks are being waged against you and knowing what to do.

The majority of political attacks are subtle or covert, the whole game is to catch the other side off guard and defeat them. In order to protect yourself, you have to learn the language and then perfect the art of politics.

This can be done anytime there's people, positions, or resources at stake. Observe the power struggle between two people who are after the same position and you will see political moves being waged against each of them. Check out the world news and you will see political battles over money, oil, and other resources across the world on a daily basis. Gain a deep knowledge of the grievance process and we can make ourselves more objective when dealing with politics and people alike.

YEAR #9: COMMISSARY

When it comes to commissary, there is a saying in prison: "commissary is Necessary." When it comes to this saying, in some ways I agree and in others, I don't.

Making commissary is our ability to buy hygiene and food items with the money our loved ones send to our inmate trust fund account. We access this account with the barcode that is located on the back of our identification card. There is no limit on the amount of money that this account can hold, but no funds in this account will draw any interest.

Before we go to the window, (we stand in front of a clear glass window as they slide our requested items to us) we fill out a commissary slip which lists the items we desire to purchase if we have enough money. The walk of shame is when you give the lady your card and she slides it back to you saying you don't have money. Sometimes they take all the IDs and scan them to make sure they have money. All the cards with no money she puts into a stack and then calls out the names of the people to whom they belong. It's the true rejection of feeling like on one cares enough to send you money, the feeling of being forgotten and abandoned. This is the essence of the walk of shame.

I don't feel it's ironic that as I type this chapter, it is actually commissary day. Depending on whom the officer is running commissary determines how smooth this day will be. If an officer is working whom can think, then he will clearly lay his plan out for who will go and when. If he's working a wing with cells, he will tell everyone, "I'm starting on four row and making my way down. If you're in the dayroom when I announce your wing, then get my attention and I will allow you to go stand by your cell." If the officer can think and he's working on dorms then he will announce, "I'm starting with one bunk and ending at eighty. When you see me come in and announce I need another shot, you need to get to your bunk and get ready for me to take IDs."

If an officer can't think, I've seen fights break out. Say, thirty-five people are sitting in the dayroom, and a officer who can't think may walk up to the dayroom bars and yell, "let me get ten people for the commissary line!"

Pandemonium! Twenty people get up and rush the bars, pushing and shoving, sticking their hands through the dayroom bars trying to get the officer to get them in the line first. I once read that self-preservation was at the top when it comes to basic human instincts and, based on what I've seen when it comes to commissary in prison, I must say that I agree wholeheartedly.

Before I get into the commissary quote, I feel it's important to mention an aspect of commissary that my boy Buddy and I are thankful for. Before prison we both depended on the women in our lives to manage the household when it comes to daily things needed to keep our daily lives flowing. Small things like staying stocked up on soap, tissue, toothpaste, groceries, etc. Never was there a consciousness of the level of responsibility it took to not only manage the money that went into buying these things but making sure that every day needs were accounted for.

In prison, they don't supply you with deodorant at all, and when it comes to soap, you get only 5 small green bars per week! When I say "bar," I know in your mind you imagine like a mini bar of soap. No! This small green bar is as long as your thumb and not even half an inch thick. Long story short, if you don't budget hygiene you gone live to smell about it.

So, when it comes to life skills of stewardship, being able to manage one's daily needs in effective ways, we have the opportunity of commissary to thank for this skill. I say opportunity because it would be foolish to give the commissary system credit for the mindset of stewardship. The opportunity of commissary gave us the platform we needed to cultivate needs versus wants, money management mentality, the art of giving and receiving, and confidence in our ability to manage our daily affairs once we are free in the physical form.

This is why when it comes to the motto, commissary is necessary, I can agree in the deeper sense of teaching one how to manage finances, develop a heart of giving, and a needs-before-wants mentality. In a shallower sense, hygiene is a must, and the fact that the last meal they feed is around 5 PM, and breakfast is fed at 2 AM is tough on a grown man's stomach. That's a big lapse in time before meals, around about 8PM, when everyone spreading (cooking), your stomach gone sound like the rumble in the jungle (smile).

The aspect of necessity that I disagree with is one that most would fail to admit that commissary is used for. This is the dynamic of commissary used to fuel self-worth. We like to call these dudes commissary kings. When these dudes come through the doors with their bags, it's showtime. Instead of going straight to their cell to put their stuff up, they'll drop the bag in front of the dayroom as if to say the bag is to heavy, they needed to take a break. Then they may ask one of they boys do they want a soda and then proceed to have to dig way down deep past all they stuff just to hand they boy the soda. This same dude, if his money doesn't hit, meaning his family didn't' send money in time for store, his whole attitude and countance is off.

On the dorms those whose self-worth is tied to what is in their locker, how much commissary they own, can easily be observed on commissary day. Those with this mindset who have no money, have their heads down in their bunk, the look on their face says, "Give me something to help me feel loved and valued, anything." The dudes with this mindset who have money and use commissary as a badge of honor, use those with nothing as pawns. While everyone sitting in the dayroom, they will notice someone who is sad cause they couldn't make commissary and announce loud, "Hey, Bro! You need something? I got plenty stuff over there if you need something, just come ask." The dude who feels like he needs things in order to feel value, will pull up, walk up to, the commissary kings cubical later reminding him of his offer and the commissary king will hand him a soup and send him on his way. This move further damages the fragile ego of the commissary slave, those who need commissary to feel worthy, deepening the mental penitentiary that confines them.

In society, we see this dynamic every day in men who use money, cars, clothes, and titles to fill a void where self-worth should be. Facebook ballers can easily be found flashing a stack of money for likes or a diva posing in the latest heels with the purse to match, starving for attention through these things. It seems that we become slaves to this mentality as a product of the superficial society that we are formed in. Those who grow up in poverty are shunned and those who have things are valued and praised. In these early stages, content of characters is rarely used to gauge value. As adaptive animals, we see this pattern of survival when it comes to mental peace and we adapt this thinking ourselves. Most of us remain stuck in the prison of this mentality, needing things outside of ourselves to fill us and make us feel loved and accepted. A few of us break free from this prison of outside validation and learn to look within and build a foundation that holds the pinnacles of our value and self-worth.

Add to the social influence, of our nature as hunter-gatherers that we get from our ancestors. The hunters who brought back the most meat and skins were seen, in the eyes of women, as the best potential mates. Those who didn't have any food or skins were seen, in the eyes of women, as unable to provide for potential offspring. The men who had the most were having the most kids, they then passed along their hunting skills and mentality of how to ensure reproduction to future generations. Women back then didn't care what your dreams were, they didn't care about compatibilities, or even how well you understood her feelings. If you could provide, you were desirable.

Fast forward over a hundred generations and this basic way of operating is still responsible in evolutionary terms for us feeling that we need things outside of ourselves in order for others to value us. Since we are pack animals, when others don't' value us, it is hard for us not to feel like something is wrong with us. The most amazing aspect about this knowledge is the fact that we know the principle! You hear it in songs all the time, Mike J. Jones said, "Back then y'all didn't want me, now I'm hot, y'all all on me." In 1998, Jay-Z and DMX dropped a song called *Money,*

Cash, Hoes that talked about this premise. Lyfe Jennings took the opposite route in his song, *Must Be Nice*, talking about the rare woman who "even when your hustlin' days are gone, she'll be by your side still holding on." In many of these songs, especially the rap songs that talk about money and hoes, the superficial mindset of being valued for what you have is perpetuated over and over again.

Buddy and I both fell into this mental trap even more because we grew up in families who struggled financially and we saw, firsthand, the influence and love those who had money seemed to have. Buddy talks about the time growing up in Louisiana. He was in Mary Poppins Apartments and he saw the whole cash money team pull in and everyone went wild. In that moment, Buddy said to himself, "I want that power."

The outside of self-system of validation was first solidified from my early school days. The first day of school was like a fashion show. Everyone was celebrated for their new J's (Jordan's), clothes, and matching backpack. With my dad in prison and my mom on drugs, my source of clothes were Salvation Army and donations. We can say what we want about our kid, but kids can be cruel when it comes to hurting your feelings. I learned the hard way, people value you when you have certain things. In our minds this was just the way it was, and at that time the things that we possessed equaled self value. How could we believe anything else?

Then I came across a quote that said, "We are not trapped by a difficult past life any more than we are by a difficult childhood," and I started to understand that I wasn't trapped in that way of thinking, that my higher power was sending me signs that true self-worth comes from a place that is deeper and more profound than the things that we have or possess. A revelation was on the edge of my consciousness, attempting to transform the source of my value.

One day Buddy then showed me a story that no one knows who wrote but is very powerful. It changed my life when it comes to my perspective of where my true value comes from:

Once a powerful executive went on vacation, his first in fifteen years. As he was exploring a pier in a small coastal fishing village, a tuna fisherman docked his boat. As the fisherman latched his boat to the pier, the executive complimented him on the size and quality of his fish.

"How long did it take you to catch these fish," the executive asked.

"Only a little while," the fisherman replied.

"Why don't you stay out longer and catch more," the executive asked.

"I have enough to support my family's needs," said the fisherman.

"But," asked the executive, "what do you do with the rest of your time?"

The fisherman replied, "I sleep late, fish a little, play with my children, take a siesta with my wife, and stroll into the village each evening, where I sip wine and play guitar with my friends. I have a full and busy life."

The executive was flabbergasted, "I'm a Harvard MBA and I can help you. You should spend more time fishing. With the proceeds, you could buy a bigger boat; a bigger boat would help you catch more fish, which you could sell to buy several boats. Eventually, you'd own an entire fleet, instead of selling your catch to a middleman, you could sell directly to the consumers, which would improve your margins. Eventually, you could open your own factory, so you'd control the product, the processing, and the distribution. Of course, you'd have to leave this village and move to the city so you could run your expanding enterprise."

"The fisherman was quiet for a moment then asked, "How long would building this enterprise take?"

"Fifteen, twenty years. Twenty-five tops."

"Then what," the fisherman asked.

The executive laughed, "That's the best part. When the time is right, you'd take your company public and sell all of your stock. You'd make millions!"

"Millions? What would I do then," the fisherman asked.

The executive paused for a moment, "You could retire, sleep late, fish a little, play with your children, take a siesta with your wife, and stroll into the village each evening to sip wine and play the guitar with your friends."

The fisherman just stared at the executive. Shaking his head, the executive bade the fisherman farewell. Immediately after returning from vacation, the executive resigned from his position.

It's like after reading this story my soul exhaled after many years of holding its breath. I realized that true value didn't come from having money, I was no longer under pressure to have to make millions in order to have value and love for myself, nor did I need things for others to value me. True value comes from loving yourself first and knowing what is important to you. Having things come from self-love. When you love yourself, that energy becomes a part of your attitude and way of thinking. This way of thinking attracts back to you the very things you desire and hold important in your heart.

A wise man once said it this way, "Maybe life wouldn't be so hard if people stopped searching for blessings and started using the ones they already have." Some say that we live in a world where we don't know what we want and we're killing ourselves to get it! I agree and know that those in the marketing business prey on our lack of understanding what we really need and want. Magazines, commercials, and social media ads are filled with the subliminal messages telling us that we are unsatisfied and if we had this product, or that person, or went on a vacation, we would feel like the smiling actors in their ads. This bombardment breeds within us discontent, this discontent then gives birth to us taking for granted the many blessings that surround us on a daily basis. Blessings that people in less fortunate countries risk their lives daily for. Things as small as being able to take a fresh shower daily or being able to worship in whatever manner that you choose without the risk of death. Without understanding what your core values are and making a decision to stand firm like the fisherman, we will continue to kill ourselves mentally, emotionally, and remain in self-imposed prisons.

The keys to unlock the doors of these self-imposed prisons are within each and every one of us. Within you are the answers that will set you free from the pressure of feeling that money, commissary, or any form of outside validation will complete you in some way.

When we slow down enough and pay attention to the unrest within our souls that tells us something isn't right, we then start to notice evidence of truth of the lack of power that money has in serving as the inner foundation of worth. We start to look closer at the lives of Robin Williams (1951-2014) and Kurt Cobain (1967-1994) and see evidence that having fame and fortune doesn't equal automatic inner peace. Both of these great men were at the top of their game when their inner turmoil led them to take their lives. Both Michael Jackson and Prince died from drugs. If having things could serve as a replacement for self-love and worth, the question remains is what were they trying to escape from? No one can enter the minds of these great men to truly understand what they faced before their deaths. The point we make here is simple, money didn't save them!

What did the fisherman know that the executive and these other great men seem to not know? When the executive attempted to urge him towards more money, what was it inside of the fisherman that knew he already had what the executive really needed?

If we look closely at the fisherman's answers to the executive, most of the time he simply said, "...and then what?" By using the Socratic method, he posed a powerful question in order to help the executive find the answer within himself. In the end, a look was all it took from the fisherman for the executive to know he'd found the truth to what really gave life its meaning. The fisherman understood what he valued most and what was important to him versus what the world tries to tell us we need to be whole, and then what should be our motto before we decide to pursue a course of action in our lives. With the end in sight, we have the insight to dissect the action and lay it next to our core values, we can measure its cost and ask ourselves if the course of action will add or take away from what we hold most important in our lives. This is why it is vital to have a vision for your life. Your vision is the roadmap for your life. It shows you where you are and what road needs to be taken in order to reach your destination. Even when we reach roadblocks or construction sites along the journey, our roadmap/vision will show us a different road in order to get back on track and headed in the right direction. Without vision, we don't know where we are going. Anyone can show up and say, "Hey, I think you should go that way, the road is smoother that way and everyone is taking this path." Most end up taking this path because they are just trying to go somewhere different than where they are in their lives. With nothing to keep them on course, the many detours keep them going in circles. Like the children of Israel, many die still haven't ever reached the destination they started out on because of a lack of vision. With your vision solid in place, you are grounded in a direction, you understand what you value, and the daily obstacles that present themselves while on the path of our journey are looked upon as exciting challenges that add strength and character to our souls!

My grandmother used to always tell my pops that when he died, he couldn't take anything with him, especially the material things. When I got older, I wondered what you could really take, but deeper than that I came to understand that what one leaves is more important than what one takes. I still haven't figured out what we take, but leaving a legacy of love, giving, and forgiveness is more important than the material things we plan to leave.

When we look at the things that truly bring peace, love, and joy to our lives we find that money is shallow. The deeper things that fulfill us are simple, but deep:

1.   "It is not good for man to be alone." This saying from the bible speaks of a core need within all of us. When we look at the story of the fisherman, we see that his life was surrounded with the people he loved and who loved him the most. In psychology, this is called our social disposition. It is because of this natural disposition that we seek out companionship and the approval of others in our lives. Even if one had all the money in the world, without others to share it with, it would be meaningless. Even on a superficial level, money would be meaningless without the praise and recognition that it gives one. The connections we make on our journey are vital to our peace, love, and joy.

2.   "Having a sense of purpose." Without this, we feel lost. Life seems somewhat meaningless and empty. When we connect with our natural gifts and talents, and we find what makes us feel alive, then we go from just being alive to actually living.

3.   "Giving back." If living out our purpose and having the people we love around us is the cake, then the icing has to be giving back. When we think about enlightenment, and the few men and women who have attained it, Jesus, Buddha, and many others, this enlightenment was not attained for themselves, but for others. To give back is to love others and to love others is to love thyself. True value comes from within first, and then sharing that value with family and friends, and then the world.

These foundational principles are how we escaped the false truths that money defines self-worth and value. "Life is not that complicated. You go to work, you eat three meals, you take one good shit, and you go back to bed. Where's the fucking mystery?" –George Carlin

KEYS TO FREEDOM

When I first hit county, I had a few thousand left to my name, with commissary and the phone being so expensive, it didn't take long for me to realize that I was going to eventually run out of money. I was in a tight spot, in a different environment, with no connections and still facing some serious time.

In society, I knew if everything failed while hustling, I could always find a job to support myself. It would have been a tenth of what I was making as a dealer, but I would have still been able to maintain. For the first time in my life, I was forced to confront myself. I had grown into a mindset of where the tangible things I had owned had become a part of my identity. Now, without any of the things I felt that made me, I started to evaluate myself a lot differently.

With this self-evaluation brough to mind was that I was compensating for my lack of formal education with material items. I felt that if I had a foreign car that I had somehow made it, but in reality, I still had a long way to go. Thus, my journey to self-mastery began. With time, I figured out true wealth and prosperity comes from within and I would never be caught up in 'keeping up with the Jones" again.

True wealth is not an amount of money, it is a state of mind.

YEAR #10: REC

Before I came to prison, the way old prison movies portrayed the recreation (rec) yard had me feeling like "Hell nall!" In those old movies, the rec yard was a place that was dangerous and segregated. Each gang had its own area that it ruled and at any moment a riot could break out over the slightest misunderstanding. Tear gas and rubber bullets were a normal part of the daily life on the yard in these movies.

Maybe in the early days, all the way up to the 90s, this was the norm, but by the time Buddy and I came into the prison system in the 2000s, the rec yard had changed significantly. Depending on the unit you are on, the rec yard can still be tense at times, but for the most part, today it is used as a place to release personal tension, walk in the raw fresh air and meditate, or workout.

On any given day on the rec yard today you might see segregation but not motivated by racism or gang life but natural segregation that comes from people surrounding themselves with people they share the same culture with.

On the basketball courts you will mostly see black men playing like scouts are watching from the bleachers. Imagine a bunch of competitive men playing basketball with hood mindsets and no ref! I stopped playing basketball and dominoes my first year down. It's a jungle.

Over on the handball court you will mostly see Mexicans going at it with all their might, bragging rights on the line. Some releasing frustration by slapping the little blue ball and imagining that the ball is the face of the latest guard who pissed them off.

On the weights, it is a mix of everyone throughout the day. Whites, blacks, and Mexicans alike use weights as a way to release built up tension and build up their bodies. For the most part, everyone is considerate of sharing each station and working together. The motto is, 'there is enough money for everyone.'

So often in life, we take the small things for granted. Until we lose them, we sometimes hardly even notice them. Coffield is an inside unit for the most part. An inside unit is a unit where for the most part, everything is on the inside of the building like chow, school, etc. On these types of units, the only time you get to go outside is at rec.

The liberation of fresh air was lost on us when we were free in the physical form. Buddy and I both took it for granted. I mentioned earlier that we are workout partners, and most days the first thing we do when we go to work out is walk in the freshness of the air and just breathe, contemplate, and exhale. For many in this life we live, the past is constantly present in our thoughts and actions. The future for us is constantly on our minds— "Will I make it out there?" "Man, I can't wait to…," and so many what ifs? But just walking and being in the moment, in the now, is so liberating. Appreciating the essence of being alive, the beauty of creation, feeling the sun beam on your face, watching the birds soar through the air, and just feeling the oneness with nature is a consciousness that we had to develop. Just being takes so much weight off of your shoulders, it is an amazing feeling.

We both strategically worked our way outside to the dorms so that we could have more availability to going outside. Being able to just go out the front door and walk onto the rec yard wasn't always a way of life for us. Inside the building, where the cells are, rec is not a regular part of the schedule. As a result, fresh air is not common.

I was in the building for six and a half years and only had the privilege of feeling the sun on my face maybe twenty time a year! In six years, I went outside about one hundred twenty times for two hours! The reasons for them not calling rec varies from them having a shortage of staff showing up for work, the weather outside being too cold or too hot, and then rec restrictions of not being able to go to rec because of a case.

Not being able to go outside and inhale the fresh air or run and lift weights builds up in the psyche. All this build-up with no way to release causes you to be frustrated, stagnated, and unfocused at times. This is why it is vital that rec is a mindset and not something that you wait to be given to you!

Out in society, the equivalent to rec would be R&R&R, rest, relaxation, and release. In American society, this is rarely given or taken as well. Growing up in my family, a vacation was two days off. While taking those two days off, there is a side hustle, the grind doesn't stop.

Fifty, sixty, seventy-hour work weeks in America is a norm. The lure of overtime checks and more money is just too good to pass up. The pursuit of things fuels our relentless focus on the grind. With most of our energy given to our jobs, we come home empty, frustrated, and exhausted. Nothing really left in the tank to give to the people who we say mean the world to us.

Having a healthy work ethic in itself is a must. In Proverbs 13:4 it says, "The soul of a lazy man desires, and has nothing..." Desire without work leads to poverty, and crime.

On another level, our work adds to the meaning of our lives. In surveys done on people who have retired, 47% say that after the first couple of years they feel almost lost, bored, and unsatisfied. Many end up starting over careers or even going back to their old jobs to fill the void. Work in a balanced life plays a significant part in how we spend our time and the people we meet. Coworkers become like second family.

The problem in America is not that we work, but we don't go to rec. Even on our day off, most of us are doing more work. Maintaining the things and the lifestyles that we have created pressure us to keep up. 'Keeping up with the Jones" has our eyes puffy and our souls depleted of the energy needed in other areas of our lives.

In psychology there is a term called 'conspicuous consumption' which means the acquisition or display of expensive items to suggest that one is wealthy. This infatuation of ours to present ourselves as successful has most of us burnt out and tired. We are constantly pouring out but putting nothing back in.

A wise man once said, "Life, like a mirror, never gives back more than we put in." Because we don't find the time in our lives for daily rec, we are drained of our mental, emotional, and spiritual energy. 'GIGO' in the computer world is an acronym for 'garbage in, garbage out.' Meaning whatever you put into the computer is what you will get out of it.

This concept applies to our lives when It comes to not taking out time to rest, relax, and recharge. When you are overworked, stressed, and frustrated from your daily grind and lack of rec, you will give this type of individual to your friends and family in return. If a cellphone is not charged up, what happens to it? Yes, it dies.

Rec does not have to be a vacation. It doesn't even have to be a weekend trip with the family on a camping trip. No, rec is a mindset that starts within and Buddy and I learned this lesson through the fires of prison life.

We mentioned earlier in the book of how Buddy had conquered death while in solitary confinement. He had learned how to use the darkness as a tool of transformation and growth.

Upon entering the prison system, Buddy was still hungry for change in his life and was looking for other areas he could improve on. Coming into prison, Buddy weighed 155 pounds soaking wet. At 6'2", he had a tall, slim build. Whenever they would call rec, Buddy would go out too clear his head for the most part. He wasn't really a baller, handball didn't interest him at all, and so one day he went over to the weights to see what all the hype was about. He jumped up on the pull-up bar and fell in love. It was if the pain from the struggle was releasing something within him, he and the pain understood one another and knew that if they just stayed in the darkness together that it would transform him.

"Gotta go to dark places" became his motto for his workouts. He connected to working out almost in a spiritual way. It had so much in common with real life. Just as in life you had to see where you wanted to be, when it came to physical training you had to have a vision of where you were going, what you would look like in the end. In life, you had to have the drive, determination, dedication, and a dream. It was the same when it came to working out. Just as in life, the darkness and pain that we face helps to release us from mental and emotional prisons; the workouts released stress and built-up tension from his soul. Never would he smoke weed again, he had his new drug.

Within six years, Buddy went from 155 lbs. to a staggering 215 lbs. Exercise served to show him a spiritual truth—when we see something in our mind and heart through faith, and mix this faith with hard work, results follow.

James 2:20 in the bible says, "But do you want to know, O foolish man, that faith without works is dead?" This spiritual truth translated into his life and a double portion. Not only had working out strengthened the principle of vision in his life, but it gave him a vision for his life— personal training. He knew working out could do the same for others like himself who had drive.

They say there are only two mistakes one can make along the road to truth—Not going all the way and not starting at all. Buddy started with a vision, went all the way, and transformed. It all started with him taking time to go to rec to clear his mind. This is why we say that rec doesn't have to be a long extended vacation or a camping trip with the fam. Rec could be the fifteen minutes you use to meditate in your car before going into work, a thirty minute gym session early in the morning or late afternoon, even walking your dog.

Rec, in essence, is any activity that gives you a break and/or helps you release pent up tension and anxiety. A lot of individuals in prison attempt to wait until rec is given to them, which is rare, and find themselves built up with frustration and anxiety. When rec is a state of mind, you give yourself rec.

I mentioned earlier that I spent six years in the building. Coffield is an inside unit and for the most part, rec is outside. There is no afternoon rec in the building, you will either go early in the morning or at night. Most of the time, they don't like to call night rec, so your best bet is to try to go early.

Morning after morning I would get up at 4:30 am. If you want to go to morning rec, you have to be in the dayroom by 5:00 am. If they are going to follow through with rec, then they usually let us out at around 6:00 am and then bring us back in before 8:00 am count time. Out of the seven days a week, you were blessed by the Almighty if you got to go to rec three days. The other days were so frustrating, a total waste of my time and energy. Some weeks would be so bad that we would only get one day. I found myself starting to gain weight because of inactivity, I was short and irritable with my homies, this even led me to having a couple of fights. One was with my very own workout partner.

Sitting in the dayroom one day frustrated, this old-school white man noticed me and asked what was wrong. I said, "These hoes don't never call rec, school. They be hatin' cause we trying to look like something."

School chuckled, "I hear you, youngster," he continued, "I once read a quote that read, 'people are always blaming their circumstances for what they are.' I don't' believe in circumstances. The people who get on in this world are people who get up and look for the circumstances they want, and if they can't find them, they make them."

I shook my head in frustration, now thinking that school might be half crazy. "How the hell am I going to make them give me rec? What am I going to do, make the dayroom a rec yard," I said.

School just smiled and looked me in the eyes, turned back to his book and continued reading. I sat there in my frustration for a minute contemplating what I just said. Something within my spirit was telling me that I was onto something; a new revelation was budding within my conscious mind. Then it hit me, I can give myself rec. I had been waiting on a circumstance that was out of my control instead of creating my own.

Using my frustration as fuel, I stood up in the dayroom and removed my state shirt (TDCJ issued) and pants and did some stretches in my t-shirt and shorts. I went into an intense burpee routine and mixed in a few sets of jumping jacks. I saw school glance over at me and smile. He knew I had made the transition and, in that moment, I had escaped the limitations of circumstantial thinking. After my cardio routine, I finished up my workout with ten sets of 50 pushups. The next day when they canceled rec, I was ready with a curl bag. Other dudes who had been as frustrated as I had been started to join in with me as we motivated each other to get paper (go hard on the workout).

Rec became a mindset! No longer did I allow circumstances to stop my growth and leave me stagnated in frustration. I gave myself the circumstances that I needed, no matter how long it took me to create them. Never again did I have to wait on a condition in order to be my best. My best was a part of who I was, and this way of thinking left my mind and created exactly what I needed to break free and overcome. Not only did it help me break free from my mental limitations but my example showed others around me the power of creating your own circumstances, thus setting yourself free from the limitations the world and other people will forever try to impose upon you, your goals, and dreams.

This way of thinking and operating is vital when it comes to creating opportunities to rest your mind and body in this world of relentless pressure. Finding unique ways to rest and recharge has become a way of life in order for us to protect our mental, emotional, and spiritual energy and creativity.

Trying to drive a car with dim headlights at night is dangerous and can lead to life altering accidents. It is clear that the battery of this car needs a charge. If smart, the owner of the car will remove the battery and take it up to the shop to rest on the charger for a few hours.

Just like the batteries of cars, we are constantly drained and driven by the world and it is vital that we remove ourselves and find moments throughout our lives to rest and charge up. The difference is instantly noticeable when the charged battery is put back into the car—sharp, bright light illuminates the darkness and allows you to navigate to your destination.

When this battery is neglected, pushed harder, and uncharged, not only do the lights begin to dim but the starter starts to drag. I think we have all inserted the key into the ignition, turned it, and heard the car fighting to start. Again and again, we have to turn the key over before we get the car to finally start period from here, it's downhill and one thing starts to affect the other. We are the same.

When we are drained, unrested, overworked, and mentally numb, it gets hard for us to even start our day. Coffee no longer works to get us stimulated, we drag throughout our workdays and come home to unsatisfied partners who are suffering from the effects of our drain. This stress causes us to feel more drained, and the fog causes us to feel down and in some even depressed. This depression then leads to health issues and so on.

In psychology there is a proven belief that our thoughts and feelings influence our brain. The nature of these thoughts determines how effective our immune system is at fighting off diseases. In essence, what we can say based on these facts is that when we are drained and stressed, we expose ourselves to health issues. Headaches, hair loss, heart disease, and weight gain can be signs that we need rec in our lives. Signs that we need to recharge, a release of tension. Release and rest through rec and meditation keeps our minds from triggering the release of stress hormones that affect our immune system. The health benefits alone should motivate us all to take hold of the power that we have to find unique ways to give ourselves rec.

Again, rec doesn't have to be an official vacation; for a lot of us our circumstances don't afford us this luxury. When rec is a mindset, we are free of circumstance and we can give ourselves a vacation by taking a long drive with the windows down, allowing the fresh air to soothe our mind. Rec is a 30-minute jog around the block to loosen up before a long day, rec is what Jamie Foxx gave himself in the movie *Collateral*. Clipped to the inside of his sun visor was a picture of the Caribbean Islands. Throughout the day, he would pull the visor down and just dream of the day he would really be there. His vision made the grind of the day all worth it, his dream kept him from getting caught up in the stress and feeling of being overworked.

When you give yourself rec like we learned to do here in prison after they cancelled rec so many times, it's vital you do something that works for you. Something that allows you to release the clutter and stress in your mind, something that gives you joy and motivates you.

In the Bible in Proverbs 17:22, it says that, "A cheerful heart is a good medicine, but a downcast spirit dries up the bones." When you find a method of rec that rejuvenates you and brings you joy, you have found a good medicine that will keep you healthy and fresh.

Buddy finds a time throughout the day to put his ear plugs in, lay back on his bunk, and gather his thoughts. With his thoughts in order, he has freed up energy and relaxed himself enough to be his best in other areas of his life.

Reading and exercise are my go-to methods of release and having a good friend to talk to in order to get a different perspective, or just vent, is a powerful form of relax and release. Most important is finding what works for you and taking the time to give yourself the rec you need to feel refreshed. When we say 'take,' that is exactly what has to be done— "to bring into one's possession by force!" The world will forcefully attempt to take your energy and so you must make it your duty to be intentional when it comes to recharging your mind, body, and spirit.

We know too well the natural wear and tear that this life has on all that inhabit it. Energy dissipates. As we get older our energy fades, with use batteries drain and die, toothbrushes lose bristles and needs to be replaced, even the sun's energy dies down throughout the day. This natural decline is called the force of entropy. It's what the second law of thermodynamics is based on.

What's amazing is the power of the human spirit to rest and recharge and defy the natural flow of entropy through mental, physical, and spiritual rejuvenation. Also understanding how still to be good stewards to the time and energy we have been given, is vital to rest.

Caterina Fake said something that was wise, "So often people are working hard at the wrong thing. Working on the right thing is probably more important than working hard."

Knowing how to give yourself rec is a vital skill in and of itself. The key is knowing that choice at any moment. On the flip side of that same coin is making sure that you are protecting your energy and using your mental focus wisely.

"He who knows others is learned; he who knows himself is wise." –Lao Tzu

KEYS TO FREEDOM

Whenever rec was called, I made it my mission to go out and get the fresh air but I still hadn't developed a purpose for going out. The first few months in prison are the most challenging for most men, I wasn't an exception to this fact. With so many influences fighting for one's attention its easy to get caught up in the prison culture.

'Rec' became a deterrent for me, a way to avoid the negative energy on the dorm. King explained how I fell in love with working out to the point that it became my new drug, it became a 'way of life for me', something that I didn't wait to be 'given' but something that I took for myself. I noticed that the people that waited on rec had a disposition for 'waiting' on everything. When it came to 'doing time' the fight had been knocked out of most men. They had never developed the 'lion mindset' that goes to war for the things it wants from life. I 'took' rec for myself because I had found the key: Rec is a state of mind and when you obtain this state of mind you obtain a certain level of freedom. Freedom from stagnation, waiting on permission, and allowing others to stop your forward momentum! 'Release' yourself though rec!

YEAR #11: VISITATION

It's the weekend. An officer opens the door into the dorm and calls out your name for a visit. "Bunk 175- Bowen for visit. Let's go, your family waiting." Immediately butterflies flap their wings inside your stomach. Your mind begins to wonder who it may be as you start the visit routine.

Step one: You got to get your hygiene right. You wash your face really good and hit the grill, brush your teeth, really good. A little water and grease help to get your waves hitting a little harder, or just to give your hair or head that shine

Step two: Back inside your cubicle, you rub down with some smell-good lotion from the hygiene pack off commissary. On top of that you rub on a thin layer of Vaseline to give your skin that glow.

Step three: It's time to pull out the tight whites, clean and starched state-issued clothes. Once dressed, you slide on either your boots or your shoes, depending on the look you're going for. Before you walk out you make sure you have three things: your ID, a Cologne strip that you wipe on right before you walk into your visit, and a piece of fruit candy that you pop in and chew for that first kiss (smile). You ready to go!

The walk over to your visit is full of excitement. As you walk, you do your best to clear your mind of the darkness that prison tries to submerge you in. You leave behind the weight of doing time and the emotional tax it charges.

You walk in to visit, get a glimpse of your kids and wife, and you're no longer in prison. The hugs from your family gives you pure joy, their smiles light up your soul, and instantly recharges your depleted energy. As you taste the sweetness of your wife's lips and squeeze on her softness, you're conscious that the kids are waiting and so you give her just enough to let her know that you still got it and she in trouble when you get home (smile).

For two hours your world is perfect. You soak in and appreciate every moment not knowing when you'll experience this again, but at the same time knowing that you will never get these moments back. This is your opportunity to create memories, to impart lessons, and to simply love.

You're in a complete bubble of bliss, time doesn't seem real, you hardly noticed the people around you. You are lost in the smiles, drowning in love, and blind to reality. Then everything changes.

The guard walks over to the table, gently knocks on the table shattering your love bubble and says, "You have five minutes left, wrap it up." For a moment everyone gets quiet, instantly realizing the reality of the situation. A slow sadness creeps inside your soul but you are aware that your energy is contagious, especially to your kids, and so you remain stoic. You smile and say it's time to pray.

You hold back tears as your family asks God to release you and to keep you safe until that time comes. Your kids ask God if you can come home with them and you fight even harder to control the tears that threatened to spill. Everyone's eyes are a shade redder as y'all stand for goodbyes, or better yet, 'see you later,' and hugs and kisses. You save 'baby' for last as you look each of your kids in their eyes and impart words of encouragement and love. You make sure that they can feel the strength of your love in your hugs. As you hold your wife in your arms her tears fall to your shoulders. Yes, you go back to a physical cell, but she is in one made up of loneliness; these moments, she never wants them to end.

One last hug for everyone, a passionate kiss for baby, and as y'all each walk back to reality of missing one another, you steal glances until you can't no more. On the way back to the dorm you make a decision not to stress over the reality, but to appreciate what you just experienced. As you enter the dorm and take in the energy of the place, the stark contrast hits you and for an hour or two you just have to lay down and close your eyes. With your eyes closed you realize the power of love; never again will you take for granted the people that mean the most to you. Every moment that you get you will make the most of it and make sure that they can feel your passion and presence.

It's our hope that this lesson that we learned from the pen can set you free from the trap of taking for granted those special moments with the most important people in your life.

We all know and understand that not one of us can escape the reality of death. Any moment can be our last period no one knows if it's the last kiss, hug, or "I love you." This reality seems to evade us today out in society. We are so self-absorbed and busy with what's important to us that by the time we step foot in the door we have little left to give to our loved ones.

When the kids rush up to you with excitement on accomplishments that they are proud of, you give them a weak smile and a thumbs up and keep it moving. Again and again you tell your wife that date night will have to be another time. When it comes to making love you're just not in the mood, too much on your mind, "tomorrow," you say in a sleepy half energized voice.

It seems as if our own self-interest and desires blind us to the blessings that are right in plain view. Not once does it cross our minds that these moments could be our last with those that we say we cherish the most. GK Clarkson said, "The only way to love something is to realize it might be lost." Our selfishness blinds us to the reality of this truth. Even when we are conscious of this truth, we justify and make excuses as to why we are too tired to invest the proper time and appreciation when it comes to the ones, we say we love the most.

Clarkson's statement rings true for a lot of men and women in prisons today. When 5 minutes are left for visit, we instantly know that this could be the last visit. Many of us have lost grandmas, brothers, aunts, children, and spouses while doing time. There is no funeral to say your last goodbyes, no family support as you grieve and try to hold onto recent memories. Visit was your goodbye and you made sure with all the passion you had in your soul to make sure they understood how you felt about them. The moment was powerful because you were conscious of the potential loss!

Is this what society is missing? Are we blinded by selfishness, self-interest, work, entertainment, and other distractions that cause us to neglect and not appreciate the special moments that present themselves to us daily? Moments that we could pause in, be in the now, and take time to cherish the blessing of family and good friends. I think Shakespeare said it best, "That is the question."

Not only can death mean that visits are our last moments with the people that we love and care for the most, our last visit with someone can come for other reasons and teach valuable lessons, also.

When Buddy caught his case, he knew it would be hard on his girl. He had met this girl when he was 13 and they had gotten serious when he was twenty. In his heart he felt that their bond would be strong enough to weather the storm that had blown into their lives like a tornado out of hell.

For the first year and a half, while he was in the county jail, she would come to visit, she had the phone on, and she was supportive mentally and emotionally. Then Buddy went to court. Fifteen years was his sentence, which meant that he would have to at least pull seven years before he would be a free man again. During conversations on the phone she seemed reserved and quiet, but overall understanding of the gravity of their dilemma.

"Visit for Walker!" Buddy knew it was his girl coming to see him. He had just told her on the phone a few days ago that he would be gone for at least seven years and he needed to see her and let her know that everything would be ok. In the county jail, there are no-contact visits. All visitation is with a glass partition between you with communication through a phone on each side of the glass.

Buddy walked in and picked up the phone and smiled a big smile at his girl, someone he thought could possibly be wifey material. She had been with him before his rise in the streets and now a year and a half into his storm, she was still there.

She picked up the phone and smiled a weak smile back at Buddy, no eye contact, Buddy noticed it right off.

"You ok," Buddy asked, concerned.

She nodded her head up and down, still no real eye contact.

"Look, I know this is as hard for you as it is for me, but we gone get through this alright. We just got to stay strong."

She mumbled something incoherent. For most of the visit, Buddy had to drag conversation out of her. Her energy was off, and she seemed distant and cold. When they stood to leave, she gave another weak smile, but her eyes told the truth. She was done, seven years was just too much for her to comprehend, the wind of the storm too strong. As she hung up the phone and walked off, Buddy knew she was gone for good. He knew in his soul at that moment that the purpose for her visit was to say goodbye.

Back in his cell, he leaned his head up against the wall and contemplated what it all meant. His emotions roller-coastered from pain, to pride, and back to 'it would be ok.' On the phone with his boy Damon, he told him to dig deep and find the lessons through the pain. Damon told him something deep, "To love and to lose is to gain."

As Buddy dug into the pain for a revelation into the lesson, he finally saw it, "The darkness will reveal the light in your life."

When you are going through the toughest times in your life, those who are the light in your life will light up the darkness. You will know who truly has your back based on their reaction to the darkness in your life. Just as fire tests gold and brings the impurities to the top, so does darkness act in the same manner when it comes to exposing who really down for you and cares for you, no matter what. This was the key, this was the lesson that Buddy took from this trial, from his pain.

This made Buddy love, admire, and appreciate the people in his life who were really down with him in a deeper manner. Now he understood that the love that they had for him was agape, the unconditional kind tested by fire. He knew the difference now.

It is our hope that the lesson that we had to learn by fire can be passed along to you without the pain. Slow down, my friend, open your eyes and truly learn to show your appreciation for the people who stand by your side in the good and bad. This is the purest form of love and it is rare.

A group of people sitting in a smelly room for a while will no longer be able to smell the stench as you and I would, just stepping into the room. In order to protect their senses from the assault on their nose, the brain will build up a tolerance, and the smell, although present, will be undetectable. Because we are constantly sitting in the room with those who love us unconditionally, their love sometimes becomes undetectable to us. We are attempting to walk into the room of your life with a fresh perspective saying: Open your eyes, undull your senses, and experience the people who love you the most.

The way that I learned this lesson was extremely painful for me. My father did a lot of time on this same unit for shooting my mother. Growing up, I vowed that I would be different from him when it came to being in my children's lives. Turns out, generational curses are extremely hard to break without knowledge, wisdom, and understanding.

When I came to prison in 2008 with a thirty-year sentence, under the new law I knew that I would have to do at least fifteen years before I could return home. At the time of receiving my sentence, my son was two years old and my daughter was eleven days old.

My children's mother at this time was in her early twenties and riding with a man in prison was a foreign concept for her to understand.

In those early days, one visit a year was a common thing and so I had to rely on pictures to see my kids grow up. Every envelope that I received and felt pictures in sent joy through my soul.

Upon opening the envelope, I would lay back onto my bunk and smile, cry, and then smile some more, all the while daydreaming and roleplaying in my head that I was there with them in the moment. I couldn't believe that they were getting so big so fast.

Then the day would come when they would call my name for a visit! My heart would start to beat fast, I would get nervous. Will they think I'm a good dad? Will I be funny? Will our conversation flow or will it be awkward and feel forced? All that really mattered to them is that I was there. That I could hold them and look them in their eyes and tell them that I was proud and that I loved them very much. Yes, I had missed the first days of school, first steps with my daughter, and losing of teeth, story time, and chasing away monsters, but in those moments at visit, I brought so much pure love and passion with me, it's as if all the things that I missed didn't matter. From the soul of my eyes, they could look within and feel and experience how much they meant to me, that's all they needed. For me to be fully present in those moments was all that mattered to them. This is where I got the key from.

Peter DeVries said something interesting that made me think. He said, "When I can no longer bear to think of victims of broken homes, I begin to think of the victims of intact ones."

Whether a home/family is intact or not is not the deciding factor in whether there is happiness, peace, direction, and love. No, what the deciding factor is how intentional you are of being in the moments with your family, fully engaged and intentional with focus on appreciating that moment and time with them, knowing that you will never get it back!

We, as prisoners, learned these virtues by fire! These lessons were seared into our souls through pain. Through escaping the pen, it is our lessons that climb the fence and creep into your minds and hearts that we hope will set you free. A gift, our way of giving back, of imparting to you wisdom that will enrich the very fabric of your lives, if only you would apply this wisdom.

Just think for a second of that special someone that you lost to what we all must face one day, death. How many times have we wished we could go back to that last moment we were with them? In our minds, we play over and over again our conversations, but this time adding in all the things that we forgot to say. We wish so much for that moment back, this time we would make the most of our time with them. Without losing the people we love, we must find a way to use deaths reality as motivation to be in the moments with those people that we love and cherish like it may be our last. A singer by the name of Jiheme has a song called *Just in Case* and in it, he's telling his girl that just in case he doesn't make it back home that night, he wants to Make Love to her like it will be their last time. Just imagine, my friend, if you made love to your woman like you would never get another opportunity, I got a good feeling a lot of her fussing would diminish (smile).

Yes, we understand that you are overworked, stressed out, and just doing your best to figure out how to make the most of work, school, and family time. Some of y'all are even trying to figure out how to get some time apart, let alone spend more time in the moment with your partner and family (smile). The COVID-19 pandemic got us all a little twisted and ready for a new normal to set in.

With us losing our loved ones at a higher and faster rate than any other time than a lot of us can remember, it is really important for us to ask ourselves what gives life meaning and make sure we are telling those that we love how much we appreciate and care for them.

In this fast-paced world we live in today, I like to break my days up into 8s. This system is not a concrete, set-in-stone, type of thing but just a guide.

The first eight is for sleep. Without the proper rest we are not going to be able to be in the moment for ourselves let alone for our friends and families. We've all seen someone nodding off in the middle of you telling them something. So do your best to get at least eight hours of sleep so that you can be alert and sound.

The second eight is for work. As Americans we spend a lot of time at work and it's unavoidable. Even here in prison, you refuse work you will be getting a case. Do your job the best you can and make sure to keep work at work! Bringing your frustration from work to your home life will only get in the way of the reenergizing energy you need from home.

Last, but certainly not least by far, the last eight is for friends and family. A lot of time this last eight hours of our day is spent running more errands, going to the gym, doing online classes to finish our degree, etc. By the time we eat dinner, take our shower, and get in the bed ready for the next work day, we have given our friends and family very little quality time. On top of that, those moments were a blur because we were trying to multitask.

Yes, it is the reality that these other things are a part of our lives and have to be done, we understand that. Here we pose a question from the Bible in Mark 8:36 that asks, "For what will it profit a man if he gain the whole world and loses his own soul?" what a powerful question. If we get done all of the things that need to be done in a day's time, what have we really done if we neglect to do the very things that feed our souls?

Do those things that will help you to achieve your dreams and the necessary things that come with daily living but do them balancing and focused on what really gives life meaning. All that we ask is that you don't take for granted the blessings that are right in front of you just because you feel you have tomorrow to do so.

The moments that we speak about to you are only real to us as daydreams, or pictures, and occasional visits. This is why we pour our souls asking that you do two things that we have highlighted in this chapter: open your eyes and be present in the moments that seem to be abundant. When you drive home from a long day at work, you walk in the door and your kid runs towards you full of love and energy, drop everything and stop in that moment and be in it. Hug your kids, kiss them, twirl them around, and make sure they know that they are what makes it all worth it. Words are unnecessary, show them by just being in the moment with them. The kids run off to play after their hugs and your wife needs her hug kiss and needs a moment to vent her frustrations. Even if you need time to unwind and get settled in before you are able to fully give her your full attention, hold her, kiss her with passion, and tell her how much you thought about her and as soon as you shower and unwind you want to hear all about her problems. Be in the moment! They only take a moment!

The next thing we ask is that you realize and not take for granted those who stick with you through the good and the bad. Those friends and family that love you agape style, make sure that they know how much they mean to you every chance you get. It is our desire to save you the hurt and heartache of ever having to experience this despair by suggesting that you embrace the meaningful people who love you in action and stand by your side. Slow down, my friend, and enjoy the fleeting moments that truly give life flavor. King B said it best, "a porterhouse steak that is dry and unseasoned is just another piece of meat," (smile)

KEYS TO FREEDOM

We are born into a world where instant gratification has become the new standard. With this perception most people feel that everything in life should come just as easy as making a phone call or ordering a product off of a smartphone. The modern world has become an endless buffet with so much to have that many never learned the power of the now. Instead of savoring moments, many just rushed past them in pursuit of a new experience.

With this sense of power at our fingertips, our relationships and careers reflect the same view and disregard to the present moment. We feel that if our careers and partners aren't in line with the things we want that we simply drop them or stay in them and become mentally, spiritually, and physically unavailable, which neither solves the problem nor brings attention to the situation. In reality, it is us and our distorted perceptions of reality.

As in most cases, this can only be solved in two ways. One, we let the culture and outside experiences dictate who we are and what is important, which always ends in life a of misery and failure. Two, we go deep within ourselves, meditate and make time for ourselves first, so that when we come out of our meditative state, we can appreciate the true beauty and shortness of life within ourselves and those around us: Take time out of each day to truly appreciate the life we've been given and make the best out of the time we have with the people we love and care about in our lives.

YEAR #12: SCHOOL HOUSE

I f you looked up the definition of schoolhouse in Webster's Dictionary, you would find that it says, "a building used as a school and especially used as an elementary school." Today it is still used to mean the same but has become a cool way of saying it.

For the most part, the prison system isn't designed to rehabilitate in any way, form, or fashion. Most men come into prison and pick up new crime skills, they are educated on how to get away the next time and meet future crime partners.

If there was one aspect of prison that one could point to and say that it represents an attempt to rehabilitate, it would be the schoolhouse. The schoolhouse is a place designed to equip you with skills that you can use to earn an honest living upon your release. For a lot of men, it shows them a level of intelligence they never knew they had, it shows them that they can take in and hold information within their minds with the best of them. This ability to start and complete things gives them confidence going into the future. It shows that they really have the potential to do other things that don't include robbing, pimping, or selling drugs.

At the basic level, a man can come into prison and get his GED. A lot of dudes who go this route and stop are motivated by looking good for the parole board and nothing more. Some get their GED and catch a glimpse of the doorway of possibility that comes through school and they take some trades.

Trades can be taken in a variety of different areas that provide a wide range of skills. A person serious about gaining some useful skills that translate into real world opportunities can get certified in skills such as heating and air conditioning, plumbing, electrician, all the way up to actual truck driving.

In the eyes of the parole board, a person who has come to prison and gained a skill is less likely to revert to the detrimental behaviors that led him down the path of least resistance in the past.

Depending on what unit you are on will determine the accessibility of each trade. In order to sign up for a specific trade that is offered on another unit, one must get on the list. This list is ordered with those who are on their way out the door as priority.

As we all know too well in the grind to achieve, one must go get everything. While waiting to be transferred, those who are serious will most likely take an alternate trade that interests him or her. The individual who has never stagnated and always moving towards the goal of transformation is said to know the difference between school and education, if only unconscious in his wisdom, by his actions.

In conventional wisdom it is said that school is an institution that pours information into its students. The student, for the most part, sits in front of the teacher and soaks in information that is given. The student sits passively as he or she takes in the teacher's way of seeing a particular topic.

When it comes to these institutions, the curriculum is already set. The student sits passively and never really learns how to think within on an internal level for himself. Because information is poured in externally, learning how to connect with their own internal voice is neglected and handicapped. This way of teaching has its benefits, but it also has its limits.

Education is said to bring forth what is already inside of an individual. Connecting him or her to natural gifts and talents within and putting one on the path to purpose. Education teaches the student to think, to take information in and use it to connect with infinite wisdom that lies within the subconscious mind. Education is not limited to a curriculum or an institution. Education is ever evolving because as people, we are ever evolving and connecting with deeper parts of ourselves.

Having the skill to (use external information to connect within) makes education powerful because it will carry you through life. School, on the other hand, makes you dependent on external information in order to find your way.

One of the greatest examples of an educator is the great philosopher Socrates. The Socratic method is famously named after him and its practitioners use very powerful questions to stimulate thinking that leads a person to the answers that lie within. His belief in internal wisdom predicated his style of educating. He believed that when you lead a person to the answer within, that revelation would sustain them in a deeper way than just pouring in information and suggestions.

His belief on how wisdom is gained was apparent when one day a man asked him about marriage. Socrates responded, "by all means marry, if you get a Good Wife you'll be happy, if you get a bad one, you'll become a philosopher."

It is our hope that out in society, the institutions that allow students to sit passively and take in information start to equip students so that in adulthood, the ability to connect with their internal wisdom isn't lacking. Some programs are going in this direction but it's our desire to see more, especially in the home.

Carl Jung, a great psychologist, once said, "who looks outside dreams; Who looks inside awakens." This is a powerful connection to the point we make. Through using methods that bring forth internal wisdom, we help those that we teach to awaken and connect with their purpose. We teach them to use information and experience as an internal compass that leads to revelation. We turn those whom we teach into passive dreamers when we ask them to look outside of themselves for purpose, direction, and answers to their personal issues.

Another form of powerful education is the art of meditation. Those who teach meditation educate their students on how to sit still, close their eyes, relax their muscles from head to toe, breathe slow, and as they exhale, they should dig into themselves for revelation, peace, or harmony. Gregory of Sinai, who died in 1346, said this about meditation, "meditation is a modern phenomenon with a long history. Sit down alone in silence. Lower your head, shut your eyes, breathe out differently, and imagine yourself looking into your own heart… As you breathe out, say Lord Jesus Christ, have mercy on me… Try to put all other thoughts aside. Be calm, be patient, and process very frequently."

What moved me about Gregory's words is how he instructs us to imaging looking into our own hearts. There is a saying that is well known, it's said sometimes as a cliché. They say, "listen to your heart." Herein lies the power of education versus school. As we look within and listen, we transcend the millions of bits of information that bombard our minds on a daily basis and we slow down, breathe, and connect to the inner wisdom that god, the universe, or your Higher Power has for us to follow. We connect to the path that leads to our purpose and clears our heads of external noise that clouds our judgement.

Some in this world avoid education at all costs because it causes one to look within and into the dark places that they want to avoid. This belief was supported by Francois Chateaubriand when he said, "We must now always try to plumb the depths of the human heart; the truths it contains are among those that are best seen in half-light or in perspective."

This type of avoiding will keep us looking outward and in constant search for answers that lie within.

I know this truth because the habit and perspective of always looking outside of myself for direction was a way of life for me. The name of the school I went to was 'get it out the mud' university. The hood that I grew up in was actually called the 'Ghettos.' All around me were signs of struggle and the reality of poverty. 'Just trying to make it,' was a way of life, and 'get it how you live,' was the mindset.

I carried this way of thinking into my teenage years and tried my hand in all types of petty crimes tryin to help my mother pay the bills and feed my younger brother and sister. The messages they were feeding me at school weren't connecting to the reality that I saw every day when I got off the bus. The teachers who stood in front of the classroom and talked never spoke about my lights getting cut off, or how my father beat my mother, which in turn led her to drugs in order to cope.

The information they were pouring into my head was useless against the embarrassment I felt when others talked about my hand-me-down things. No test they ever gave me asked me how I felt about my dad shooting my mother in her face and receiving seventy-five years, and how despite all the pain he caused, I still missed him.

In my head, school couldn't save me or my family. The external evidence to support my theory was all around me. How could it not be true if, with my own eyes, I could see it? The lessons that I needed to study were the lessons from the streets, the university of life. They were the lessons that would equip me for the life that was waiting for me in adulthood; the tests I would take would be the streets trying to test my heart.

I lived this reality to the fullest and gave my all to apply the knowledge that I had gained from 'get it out the mud.' The thing I misjudged was how much tuition would end up being. In the end, when I checked how much I owed, it said I owed 30 years with a fifteen year down payment!

If looking externally had cost me this much, then would an internal evaluation hurt? I remember seeing myself on the news. The newscaster had just finished saying that for the next fifteen years I would be behind bars and the streets felt that much more safe that another thug was safely behind bars.

In that instant, my torso started burning on the inside. I felt myself feeling drained, lightheaded, and tired. I rubbed my chest in hopes that whatever this sensation was would subside. It didn't. I lay back on my bunk in the county and I heard my own voice talking to me, giving me the game: "You okay. That burning in your chest is like your check engine light letting you know it's time to change course. From this point forward, when you feel this burning, know that a change of direction is needed. If you learn to listen to me and stop looking externally at information, I will educate you and bring forth what has been in you your whole life."

I opened my eyes and turned my head from side to side to make sure I wasn't going crazy and everyone watching. No one was watching me, and I seemed to be intact and so, I laid back and closed my eyes.

My internal voice went right back to lacing me up, "You have given most of your life to the streets based off of the patterns you have seen around you. Everything you've learned was from the school of 'get it out the mud,' and you graduated with the honor of thirty years! This is not your path."

I could still feel my hands rubbing my chest. "Your gift is discernment. You have a special gift to look inside of people and see them, to see what they are trying to hide, and to guide them. The problem is that you have been using this gift in the wrong ways. It is not by accident that you were the leader of your gang, and it's also not by accident that you started an escort service with no idea of why you were doing it. People follow you because you have the ability to see them and make them feel understood. From this point forward, use your gift to liberate people from their fears and help them to connect to their true potential, but before you can do that, you have to liberate yourself!" I asked, "how," out loud and opened my eyes to make sure again that I didn't look crazy and no one was thinking I was talking to myself.

"To liberate yourself, you must learn to trust this voice. It will guide you. Believe in your gift and be that example that you will. Gang life has to stop, get your education, and strive to be your best. Mind, body, and spirit. You have fifteen years to cultivate these skills and wisdom. Do this and your life will go to heights you never imagined, and you will shine as an example for those who are lost in the trap of using external wisdom for direction. I will guide you in every difficult situation you face in many different ways. You must learn to see it."

I sat up and realized that my chest wasn't burning anymore. The burning sensation was replaced with a powerful ball of energy. That energy went down into my body and then up to my brain. When it hit my head, I stood up and hit my head on the top bunk. "Damn," I said out loud. Now, all of a sudden people wanted to look. I saw a few dudes giggling but I was not letting nothing get in the way of my new mission.

Long story short, I was no longer affiliated with a gang before I left the county jail. I called a meeting with my homies and told them that I wanted something different and better for my life and I hope the same for them. I began to read and learn about different possibilities. The world became so big, and my vision was expanded.

I also got my education, the first in my family to hold any college, let alone two different degrees. I also found out that I was smart. My whole three years of educating myself, I only had two B's and my GPA is considered high honors. Everything that I learned from school, I applied to my calling! This is why I say I educated myself.

Bruce Lee said something profound, "all forms of knowledge leads to self-knowledge."

The school of life has its benefits, lessons, and wisdom. It's our job to take this external information and use it to develop an internal voice that will guide us to our natural gifts and talents.

Not at all do we say that school is a bad thing, our premise is that it has value but has greater limits.

Buddy realized its value when he embarked on his pursuits of education. It was easy for Buddy to identify when he was dealing with a teacher who was educated versus one who was just smart and held a lot of information about the topic they taught. Those who were educated made the lessons come to life. You could tell that they were exactly where they were born to be. They had fire in their eyes, excitement in their voices, their movement around the room was like a dance. Every lesson had real life application and they found a way to make you think.

In classes where the teachers were just smart, Buddy noticed in back and forth questions and answer sessions he was holding his own. The internal wisdom that he had gained from the hard knock academy touched on a real-life application that the shallow, smart teachers couldn't seem to comprehend.

Mrs. Smart stood before the classroom disappointed about the low grades from the last test, she was pacing back and forth giving her speech. "I gave you all a study guide and I'm really disappointed that most of you failed the test period" she was scanning the room with a frown.

Buddy raised his hand and started to speak before he was acknowledged, "ma'am, a failure is when you don't take anything from the thing you got wrong. Every day in my hood I see real people who have failed the test of life and don't get a retest or corrections like we do. I wouldn't say we failed at all, let's go over what we got wrong and grow from it."

Mrs. Smart got red in the face and wore a snarl on her face that said she was the teacher, not him. "Nobody is taking this test over again and there will be no correction, and that's that! When you don't study hard, you fail. Better luck next time."

Buddy waved her off, "ok, ma'am, this is your class, but you just contradicted yourself. First you say if we study, we won't fail, then you want us to depend on luck for results. We confused."

The whole class was eyeing Buddy and the teacher. "Buddy, go to the hallway this minute. I'll meet you there in a second."

This exchange was one of Buddy's first confirmations that the power of an internal education held more weight than the information that schools taught you to depend on. The experience empowered Buddy and showed him a side of himself that felt liberating, grounded, and exciting. He knew now that the pain and struggle had added a level of depth and character to him that he'd never noticed before. He had believed before that someone with formal school was on a better level than someone who got it out in the mud or education through experience. Now, he knew better.

Charles M. Schulz said something that Buddy can identify with, "Life is like a ten-speed bike, most of us have gears we never use."

Buddy now lives his life knowing that at all times he is on the path of education, using all relevant information to not only see the dots, but to connect them in a way that will reveal the true picture of his destiny.

As we spoke of earlier in the chapter, we believe that school has its value. We believe that its value is in the responsibility to equipped us with knowledge. Webster says that knowledge is, "the condition of knowing something..." We know all too well that just because we know something, it doesn't mean we act on it. This fact brings us to the unique relationship between knowledge, understanding, and wisdom.

For all intents and purposes, knowledge is simple information that is taken from external sources. A lot of the things that we are told, values that we are told to have, and the proper ways to behave, are given to us at home. Then as we enter the schooling system, we are given more information to know, which is the root word of knowledge.

To know something is the first step and is basic. Understanding is a deeper way of knowing something. I know that when I put my popcorn in the microwave and push the button that says "popcorn," that my popcorn will be finished within a couple of minutes. I still don't understand the inner working of the microwave or how the electromagnetic waves produce enough heat to cook the kernels. I may know that my girlfriend shuts down anytime I ask her about her childhood, I may not understand that her childhood represents pain and suffering, and she just isn't ready to face the darkness.

If knowledge represented a set of binoculars, then understanding would resemble represent a telescope. Virginia Woolf said this about understanding, "these are the moments of revelation which compensates for the chaos, the discomfort, the toil of living."

Understanding is the 'why,' the 'how' something is what it is. It's the ah-ha in your contemplation, the light bulb in your darkness. Understanding bridges the gap between knowledge and wisdom and wisdom enlightens you to a course of action, or not, that you can take. If knowledge are the dots, understanding would be connecting them. Wisdom would be coloring the picture or action.

In a generational family tree, if knowledge was the son, understanding would be the father, and wisdom would be the grandfather. Wisdom is the end result, it's the application of knowledge and understanding that one has accumulated throughout life.

Knowledge and understanding may clearly see the connection between smoking and cancer, but without wisdom, smoking will still take place. Wisdom is an action word, a verb, the show and prove, the results.

LaRoche Foucault said about wisdom, "Wisdom is to the soul what health is to the body." When we continually act in ways that elevate us and keep us growing, we protect our souls from the heartache and pain that comes from bad choices and decisions. Wisdom is the first cousin of education because, just as the soul lives within, so does education. It is brought forth from within.

Last but not least, it's important to know that all three of these aspects, knowledge, understanding, and wisdom, ride inside the vehicle of experience. The more we live in experience new things, the more knowledge we take in. We convert that knowledge into understanding and then we apply it to our lives. All made possible through experience. In the end, when we tie everything in together, Wisdom, Overstanding, Knowledge, Experience/education, it all means that we are 'WOKE!'

KEYS TO FREEDOM:

Growing up, like most young men from poverty, I hated school. A lot of the things that were taught in class either didn't make sense or couldn't be applied in real life. I always felt that there was more to life than taking tests and memorizing a bunch of information in classrooms. With society pushing that way of thinking, it was difficult to imagine any other way of becoming successful in life. I decided to drop out and forge my own path moving forward. I didn't know it at the time, but I had enrolled in the university of life. The streets became my classroom which meant that I had to think on a deeper level, a higher level.

As with most things in life, that choice led to a lot of other decisions. In the streets I had no safety nets, especially in the drug game. Every move was a matter of life and death. Being in the game, I became an entrepreneur, a leader, a boss, and as we all know very well in the game, your time always comes. Mine did and it led me into one of the most powerful classrooms in life, prison.

Prison changed my view of what I felt I knew about life, it forced me to educate myself on one of the most important subjects I would ever study—who I was. My education of self became spiritual, and I questioned everything that I had been taught. This journey led me to have to think and as a result, I became a thinking man.

Never forget this: education will test you in who you are, it will lead you to the knowledge of self. School will give you information that is good for external use but is limited for introspection. Look within.

YEAR #13: INFIRMARY

I magine being crowded into a large chicken pen, your vision is obstructed by chicken wire as you look through it to get a glimpse of whatever it is, you're trying to see. Sitting next to you on iron benches, other men cough and scratch and fidget around in their seats waiting on the provider to try out the next generic experimental drug on their real or imaginary ailment. This is the Infirmary on Coffield Unit.

The Infirmary is a place in prison where one goes to get treated for mental and physical infirmities. Whether your issue is medical, dental, psychological, or psychiatric, the Infirmary is your best bet. You can try your luck with what we call medicine men, men in prison who have all the pills and can tell you what is best for what, but that is a personal risk that each man has to take for himself. On the streets, the dorms and hallways of prison, one can buy just about any medication from antibiotics all the way down to non-aspirin. A lot of the time, to avoid the medical copay of $100 a year, yeah, we know, and to escape the overcrowding and long waits at the Infirmary, men choose to get their meds off the street cheaper and faster. Because of the crowded area they house us in, inside the Infirmary you can go in with a twisted ankle from basketball and leave with a cold.

In order to gain access to the Infirmary you must fill out either an I-60 or what is called a sick call. A sick call is a form that asks you the nature of your issue, your personal information, and the date. With your signature, you are agreeing to pay the copay that is involved with your treatment.

In prison they use two pills for mostly all medical issues. For any and all symptoms that resemble anything cold related you will be given a small yellow pill that is commonly called a cold Buster. For any element that is pain related, a nurse will commonly give you a pack of non-aspirins. For anything stronger in these two areas, a nurse must refer you to a provider for further evaluation. Dental is a separate department located inside of the Infirmary and they don't deal with braces, dentures, or gold crowns etc. Basic dental services include silver and tooth colored fillings, stainless steel crowns, and when needed, oral surgery. Once a year you can also get your teeth cleaned, the $100 copay covers this.

You can get out of paying this $100 copay for a couple of reasons. If someone hits you over the head with a fan motor, this is what's called a life-threatening situation. You will not be charged for the treatment you need from this assault. The same goes for if you get shanked or stabbed. Your copay is also exempt for any follow up treatment to check on your progress. Also, chronic issues that include asthma, diabetes, TB, HIV, and AIDS, are not charged this dolla for treatment.

Another common aspect of the prison Infirmary is a dynamic that we will only mention here but dig into later in the chapter. For one reason or another there is a handful of individuals who are habitually sick and every time you happen to enter the Infirmary, they are sitting there with a new ailment waiting to be seen by the doc. For some this is their hustle. Like I mentioned earlier, a medicine man is one who has a pill for everything and can sell you some for a small fee. In order to stay supplied, they must visit and endure the long process of seeing the provider or unit doctor. To maximize profit, everything they get seen for is related chronic. Others who frequent the Infirmary have a mental disposition for being sick, and as a result they manifest self-fulfilling prophecies. These individuals are considered hypochondriacs. Hypochondria is the conviction that one is or is likely to become ill, persisting despite medical evidence to the contrary. Because their minds are sick, their bodies follow.

A hospital or clinic would be considered the free-world version of the infirmary. In these institutions we find some of the same conditions that we find here in prison. Emergency rooms are filled to the breaking point and overcrowded because of the Covid-19 pandemic. The caseloads of the doctors and nurses have them overworked and at their wits end. We are in unprecedented times that has people operating in fear and uncertainty Studies on fear have revealed an innumerable amount of info that suggests that it attacks our minds ability to rationalize in an effective manner, effecting our frontal lobe, the forefront part of our brains that is responsible for our moral, ethical, and rational decision making.

Phineas P. Gage was 25 years old in September 1848 when he was working with powerful explosives at his job at the railroad. A massive explosion sent a thirteen-pound tamping rod through his head. God must have been with Gage that day because he survived the traumatic accident.

With time, he was back to speaking and doing all the physical activities that he did before, but his friends and family saw some big changes. The responsible husband, respected hard worker, God-fearing man had died in the accident. The damage to his frontal lobe had left behind a man who was short-tempered, rude, foul-mouthed, who had no respect for spiritual issues at all. Gage died 13 years after the accident and through research on his brain, his accident has led to vital information on the importance of the healthy reasoning power that lives in our frontal lobes.

Gage caused damage to his frontal lobe through a physical accident, may he rest in peace, but for most the damage to their reasoning power is done through fear. This fear enters the frontal lobe and causes it to malfunction by triggering the release of stress hormones. Through release of the hormones, it effects the way we feel and think. Some people in the hospitals we frequent today are not there because they are actually sick, the sickness they suffer from stems from character defects in their thinking.

Cousin to the word infirmary is the word infirmity. Both share the root word infirm which means "weak of mind, will or character…not solid or stable: Insecure." If the infirmary and hospitals are the "places where the infirm or sick are lodged for care and treatment," why is it that most of these places focus solely on the physical and not the weakness of these individuals' minds or their shattered will and character?

Maybe the answer lies in the fact that there is more money in hormonal pill treatments. Pills like Prozac, Xanax, Ativan, Zoloft, and Paxil are prescribed by the millions and sold worldwide, making the pill industry a multi-billion-dollar business. Keeping people in these mental prisons keeps people enslaved, and we all know that slavery has been used by the power for profits since the beginning of time. By treating the symptoms, hormonal imbalance and physical, and not the source of a person's weak thinking, business continues to flow.

If you brought your car into my shop for an oil change because you keep losing oil, and I notice a hole in your oil pan, but just add more oil knowing that you will be back in a few days, I would be doing the same thing as these doctors who focus only on symptoms and not the source.

Maya Angelou said, "Self-pity is in its early stage as a feather mattress. Only when it hardens does it become uncomfortable."

This quote brings to mind an individual who is on the dorm we live on now. Buddy and I have spoken to each other about the condition of his mind and how it is connected to his many conditions. Day after day this individual finds a new reason to be down about something. His mind is so focused in on what is missing in his life that he can't see the forest from the trees. As a result, pain and sickness attack his body daily, which in turn, gives him more things to complain about. It's a never-ending cycle. No matter how much Buddy and I have tried to teach him about the power of his mind, we are no match for the comfort that his misery gives him. Comfort from misery? Yes, his misery is all he has, and he uses it to get things; it's his hustle, his identity, and gives his life meaning. When this soft pillow hardens, he is rocked by pain and mental anguish, and then it's back at it. The cycle is set in stone.

St. Augustine said something that set men like Buddy and I on the course of knowing that the solution to our issues lived within. He said, "Men go abroad to wonder at the heights of mountains, at the huge waves of the sea, at the long courses of river, at the vast compass of the ocean, at the circular motion of the stars; and they pass by themselves without wondering."

This is a sad fact, but it is true, for most of our lives we miss out on the understanding of our mental strength and look abroad for temporary fixes that only add to our turmoil. I recently had my inner mental strength tested by COVID-19.

Because I have my mind, body, and spirit operating on a consciousness level of excellence I felt almost invincible to COVID-19. I learned quickly that there was a difference between fear and caution. I didn't fear COVID-19 and, as a result I only wore a mask when absolutely necessary. Because I work around officers in the ODR, I am exposed to more free world people than the average. My mistake at work was assuming that since all the officers were wearing masks I was good not to wear one period. Thing is, they came in with their mask on, took them off to eat, and then put them back on before they left.

Long story short, one day I woke up and a scratchy feeling was in my throat. This led to a slight cough; By the next morning, my energy level was only 45%. I was freezing in 90-degree weather and all I wanted to do was lay down and sweat it out. If you went down to the Infirmary to report that you had symptoms of COVID they were packing your stuff and sending you to seg for 14 days. If it was just a common cold that I was going through I didn't want to take a chance being put on the wing where I could really catch it. My plan was just to lay down and sweat it out.

Buddy had different plans, "Oh, so you gone lay down all day, huh," he asked.

I lifted my head from under the blanket and mumbled, "Yeah, bro, I got body aches and chills. My energy level is shot to hell."

He just stood there looking down. I did my best to scare him away by saying, "Look bro, I'm not trying to get you sick. When I shake this shit, we'll get back on our grind."

He didn't move and I was getting frustrated because I wanted to go back into hibernation. Then he said, "you can either surrender and lay down in your sickness or you can tap into the strength of your mind, get up, and sweat it out the hard way. What you gone do?"

"Are you goin' to surrender to the sickness?" I kept repeating his question in my mind. Here I was claiming the sickness, becoming one with it in my mind, and allowing it to control the show. No! I was in charge, and not for one more moment would me and Covesha (COVID-19) lay in bed together, her ass had to go!

Buddy must have saw something change in my eyes because he snatched the blanket from my body and told me to get up and be ready to workout in 45 minutes. After three days of burpees, jumping jacks, pushups, and squats my energy level was up to 85%. Day five I was back to me.

Robert Frost said simply, "The best way out is always through." It's not that sickness can be avoided in our lives; it's avoiding and allowing our minds to become one with the sickness that we experience. A negative mindset can cause immune suppression, which lowers the number of diseases fighting B and T lymphocytes or white blood cells. Those who go into a cancer battle with a 'I'm going to beat this attitude,' come out survivors more times than none.

The interdisciplinary field of behavioral medicine studies how stress and unhealthy lifestyle behaviors affect our overall health. Specific to the study of mind body connection is the field of psychoneuroimmunology. There are four parts to this word that when you break them down and then bring them together, they make sense. Psycho- deals with understanding how your thoughts and feelings affect you. 'Neuro' or brain, that in turn releases hormones that affect your 'immune system'. The study, -ology, of all this makes up this field. This field and others have made some amazing discoveries as to the benefits of staying stress free, living a healthy lifestyle, and keeping a fighter spirit.

It ain't fun when the rabbit got the gun is one of my favorite sayings. It's even more fun when I got the gun and Lil bro Buddy is the rabbit. Three weeks after he snatched my covers off of me and encouraged me to get up and grind out my sickness, it was his turn! We don't wear masks when we worked out, so while we were grinding out my sickness, I was breathing hard and sweating and inadvertently passed Covesha to my boy (yea, she a thot).

I walked up to his bunk one day and he was laying there with that sick look in his eyes. "That shit on me bro. Damn."

I rub my hands together real fast like I'm warming them, "You already know what time it is," I said with an evil grin on my face, "I'll meet you at the spot in forty-five minutes."

He shoots me an evil look before I walk off to go change into my rec clothes. Payback is a bitch and I'm about to have some fun. Buddy has one of the strongest willpowers I have ever seen, he will fight to the death before he bows out in defeat. One thing I know from experience about Covesha is that she will drain your physical and emotional energy and trying to do intense cardio with her on your back takes going to dark places.

That day I put him through a burpee routine where I timed the first two sets with the aim of getting faster each set. Once I saw the average time, we were finishing I said, "Our last set will be when you take 12 seconds off this time! How long we work out today is on you." If looks could kill…well, you know the rest. That day I saw Buddy have to go to a place deep within his soul. With body aches, shortness of breath, and fatigue ravishing his body, taking 12 seconds off of the already low time was nearly impossible.

We were like five sets in when I see him pause, close his eyes, take a deep breath, and compose himself. Sweat was dripping from his body like a shower. When he opened his eyes and looked at me, I knew that this would be our last set. He took fourteen seconds off his time. I hugged him and told him how proud I was of him. Three days later he was back to 100% and he told me something that stuck with me, "Bro, Napoleon said that 'courage isn't having the strength to go on; it's going on when you don't have the strength!' Let me get that money for thinking that you was going to break me, (smile).

We laughed as I raised my arm to let him get his lick in. In that moment when he decided to have victory over his sickness, he taught me the value of living your advice; being the example of what you stand for and expecting that the principles that you say you live by will be tested. Connected to this lesson was the lesson of the power of positive friendship. Who knows how long it would have taken us to recover from COVID if we didn't' have to be accountable to one another, never allowing the other to give less than his best? Positive encouragement and motivation are a vital tool in this life we live. I learned that through my lil-bro, Buddy. Recently on National Geographic we saw a show where a young lion had wondered off on his own into hyena territory. Quickly he found himself surrounded by twenty hungry hyenas. Those in the front would distract his attention while the ones in the back took turns biting him. As the large group closed in on him, off in the distance his homeboy, who was looking for him, had finally saw him and noticed he was in trouble. Instantly he began to run over to help his boy; every hyena scattered and ran off. The help of his friend saved his life. They ran up to one another and rubbed manes and fell to the ground play fighting. Buddy and I knew how they felt, maybe we had saved each other's lives.

"When a friend is in trouble, don't annoy him by asking if there is anything you can do. Think up something appropriate and do it." –E. W. Howe

In prison and hospitals around the world, infirmaries and hospitals alike are filled with people who are really suffering from death and disease. Since the beginning of time, sickness has been a part of our world. Plagues, pandemics, and outbreaks are more than just mind-sets, they are a real struggle that are a part of this world.

What we highlight and focus on in this chapter are those who have a disposition to bring sickness upon themselves because of their mindset. Herbert Spencer once was quoted as saying that, "the preservation of health is a duty. Few seem conscious that there is such a thing as physical morality." If we allowed our character to get lazy with impatience, overweight with anger and disrespect, and sick with selfishness, we would be criticized and considered unacceptable by society; those who cared for us would motivate us to change and get better. It is our hope that soon we all will take up the duty to help those with sick mindsets as if it was our moral duty to help them change.

Whether it's noticing it within yourself or in those that you love, the signs are the same for the most part: They carry around a low countenance eighty-five percent of the time, some type of physical problem is a constant part of their lives, and problems are highlighted more than blessings. They are stress-minded and not bless-minded. Stressin not Blessin.

The type of mindset that we carry is a personal choice. Yes, we live in a difficult world with challenges. It is what it is, but at no time are there no blessings that we can't hold onto. If our brothers and sisters from the past can stay strong through Nazi concentration camps and brutal plantations, then we have no excuse today.

We cannot control the things that happen in this fallen world, but we can control our perspective. With understanding of our locus of control, we can cultivate a positive mindset that allows us to take the lessons from everything that we face. We must turn shit into fertilizer every chance that we get. We must understand, as Napoleon Hill did when he said, "The capacity to surmount failure without being discouraged is the chief asset of every man who attains outstanding success in any calling."

When we mix in exercise, meditation, prayer, and a healthy diet with this mindset, we may still face sickness, but our whole being will fight against it.

One might ask if this mindset is something that you are born with our can it be cultivated throughout time. History will show that this 'Lion mindset,' my name for it, is forged through three main aspects that we all have access to:

1. Self-belief: This is a powerful belief that you are a warrior with heart, that you have the power to decide the course of your life and overcome anything that tries to get in your way. A belief that you were born for greatness and that a power lives within you, helping guide you to your destiny.

2. Vision: Determination without direction is nothing. You must have the ability to see where you are going and be determined to stop at nothing to get there. In the movie *The Book of Eli*, Denzel Washington showed what it meant to have a vision, to know where you are going, to be guided by a power within and to stop at nothing to get there. In one part of the movie he lost The Book and got shot. In the next few scenes, you saw him back on his feet, headed west. Know where you are going!

3. Resolve/perseverance: This is the strength to keep fighting with a strong mental attitude despite difficulties. Never allowing self-doubt or setbacks to have victory over your thinking. Understanding that the whispers of failure are lies, and that through positive affirmations, faith, and a bend-but-don't-break mentality, victory is around the bend! This mindset and action are your part, the rest will follow.

KEYS TO FREEDOM

I understand this mindset of having an infirm, weak of mind, will, or character all too well. One thing about the life that we live is that it is never going to be easy. People, including myself at one time, seem to live in expectancy of this false truth. By living in this false reality, we set ourselves up for failure because the challenges never stop. When we continually get bombarded with trial after trial, tribulation after tribulation, and struggle after struggle, we become weak in our will and we conclude that since we will never make it to this promised land of the easy life, we might as well throw in the towel and give up. This is especially true when we see examples of others around us giving up their fight and passion for their chance at life instead of cultivating strong mindsets that include the three virtues that my co-author, King B, just mentioned up top—Self-belief, vision, and perseverance. I had to learn these strengths through the fire of my cell.

My first few days in seg were a real-life nightmare come true. I wasn't in my cell and hour when I heard rank and medical try to save a guy who had slit both of his wrists in what would become a suicide. As I sat back in my cell trying to process what I just experienced, I was immediately overcome with grief and sadness on a level I hadn't felt before.

Twenty-four hours later, I began to get messages from guys that were selling their meds. I never had been into pills before, so I denied all advances, but after a full year in seg, my inner resolve had broken. My girlfriend had left me weeks earlier and I was now on my way to prison to start my sentence. I decided I had enough and started collecting pills.

I took a deadly combination of pills as described in Year #5: Cell. Before that moment, life hadn't seemed like anything special, but once I realized I was dying, the preciousness of life hit me like a ton of bricks. I fought for hours to stay conscious and it was through these difficult moments where I finally woke up.

When times get tough, there will always be a thousand ways to avoid the problem, but just like treatments that never cure diseases, the disease will eventually resurface with a vengeance. The thing is to learn to cure our disease, which starts in the mind. Once we know what the disease is, we go at it head-on. This is the mentality you have to develop when dealing with ailments or life issues.

Understand, true healing is a mind state; we have to fight to keep our minds positive.

YEAR #14: CHAPEL

F our to five hundred men gather together. Some crying, some raising their hands in surrender, others clapping. In the back of the chapel some embrace for the first time in weeks, it's their first time seeing one another since they were moved off the wing. Some pass kites, handwritten notes, with carefully written instructions, while others giggle and play flirt with their lover.

In prison the Chapel is a place where most gather looking for some form of hope, a connection with their higher power, and to bond with those who believe in similar ways as themselves. In the Chapel they experience a temporary escape from the reality of prison. It's a moment to let it all go, to cry and not feel ashamed, to fill their souls with light.

Those who are there seeking a relationship use the message to connect with something within them that confirms something they have been feeling. They are using the atmosphere and the energy to vibe with the power within themselves that they have been cultivating during their walk or journey with God. They leave the Chapel with confirmation of what Jesus spoke in John 14: 12 when he said that those who believed would do greater works than Jesus himself. For this individual the church will leave with him and sustain him outside of the Chapel and help him walk in faith and not fear.

On the flip side of the same coin, some frequent the Chapel looking for religious practices to hide behind. They are in search for external stimuli to make them feel better. They believe that if they go to church a certain number of times, pray three times a day, and give their celly a soup they are holy. When gang life gets too hot, some turn to religion for safety. Others who are ashamed of their sex crimes use church attendance as a morale builder, and those who use the ego to feel important, worm their way into leadership positions in order to feed their desire for control.

The religious tend to feel that closeness to God is accomplished through deeds that others can see, when in essence, true power is a spiritual internal awakening that manifests itself through introspection and faith.

For our intents and purpose, religion is man's attempt to mimic spiritual deeds in an attempt to compensate for a weak area in their lives. Those on the spiritual journey have a relationship with their internal infinite intelligence, God, Jesus, higher power, universe, etc., and their faith in this relationship manifests itself in action. In one dynamic the emphasis is put on doing things to (look spiritual) versus the emphasis being put on faith in the power that has been (given to us) to live spiritual lives.

In our free-world churches we also find religious and spiritual dynamics. For some 'churches,' is something that is supposed to be done. Go to church on Sunday and you get a pass for the week. I know this philosophy personally; As soon as the service was over, I went to my car, my girl pulled a blunt out of her purse, and we rolled out of the parking lot getting high. Some couples smile at one another lovingly throughout the service and then get home and call each other every disrespectful name known to man. To the religious, it's all about doing (spiritual looking) things that look good.

To the spiritual church it is used as a trail that leads them into themselves to connect with the spirit of God within.

Does church lead them into themselves? Yes, into the light within, the image of God within, the spirit within. There is a story about this light within that has been used many times in different forms. This story was taken from the Hindu faith and although the Hindu names have been changed, the power of the story still remains:

Val granted Jana permission to ask him any question and Jana asked, "Val," he said, "what is the light of man?"

Val replied, "The sun, O king; for having the sun alone for his light, man sits, moves about, does his work, and returns."

Jana said, "So, indeed it is, o Val. When the sun has set, o Val, what is then the light of man"

Val replied, "The moon indeed is his light; for, having the moon alone for his light, man sits, moves about, does his work, and returns."

Jana said, "So indeed it is, O Val. When the sun has set, O Val, and the moon has set, what is the light of man?"

Val replied, "Fire indeed is his light. For, having fire alone for his light, man sits, moves about, does his work, and returns"

Jana said, "When the sun has set, O Val, and the moon has set, and the fire is gone out, what is then the light of man"

Val replied, "Sound indeed is his light, for, having sound alone for his light, man sits, moves about, does his work, and returns. Therefore, O king, when one cannot see even one's own hand, yet when a sound is raised, one goes towards it."

Jana said, "So indeed it is, O Val. When the sun has set, O Val, and the moon has set, and the fire is gone out, and the sound hushed, what is then the light of man?"

Val said, "The self indeed is his light, for having the self alone as his light, man sits, moves about, does his work and returns."

Jana said, "Who is that self?"

Val replied, "He who is within the heart, surrounded by the pranas (senses), the person of light, consisting of knowledge. And there are two states for that person, the one here in this world, the other in the other world, and as a third an intermediate state, the state of sleep. When in that intermediate state, he sees both those states together, the one here in this world, and the other in the other world. If a man clearly beholds this self as Brahman, and as the lord of all that is and will be, then he is no more afraid. Let a wise Brahman, after he has discovered himself, practice wisdom. Let him not seek after many words, for that is mere weariness of the tongue."

In his book *Outwitting the Devil,* Napoleon hill calls this connection with infinite intelligence the other self. He, too, agrees that this self transcends fear and lives through faith in the power that he has been given!

Jana immediately wanted to know more about self, and it would be wise if we used a spiritual relationship and not religion to connect with this other self also.

In Christianity this other self is called a new creation. The born-again self with a renewed mind. No matter where you look, we find the importance of connecting with a higher part of ourselves.

Stuck in a systematic way of receiving and following information, Buddy and I both hit roadblocks in religion that led us to dig deeper through soul searching to find our own path.

Once we broke free from dogmatic ways of seeing things and opened our eyes, the first thing that we saw was the diversity of God through nature. Seeing this diversity of life, we saw these same characteristics in the pursuit of humanity to connect with a higher intelligence. This motivated us to shed the labels of religion and go on a journey of connection with the part of ourselves that were made in God's image, the internal wisdom that has always been a whisper of direction out by the noise of the world. Whether you call it the other self, the Holy Spirit, infinite intelligence, or the subconscious mind, is irrelevant; connecting to this voice and power within is all that matters.

As human beings we love concepts. When we can put things in categories and make them measurable and able to be analyzed we feel better. The religious labels that we try to stamp onto God and then warn people that it is the only way to truly understand God is an attempt to make GOD a concept. Through experience we can see that these dogmatic concepts fail us in application to real life and leave us more confused than enlightened. But, as we connect to the internal power that was breathed into us, when we begin to walk in that image that we were made in, we gained wisdom navigating the trial of life in faith and not fear.

Galileo said something centuries ago that we both agree with, he said, "You can't teach a person anything You can only help him find it within himself."

We both learned this astounding truth in our own unique ways. Buddy carried many different voices inside his head for many years. Everyone from his family, his teachers, and other dudes in the streets had an opinion on what direction he should go, what he should believe, or what would be the best path for success. With all this external information coming his way he was pulled into many different ways of thinking which had him drowning and confusion and indecisiveness. In order to cope with the stress that came from being pulled in so many different directions, Buddy smoked weed like it was going out of style, at least while he was high the voices would stop, any break he could get would he would take no matter the cost.

As we know very well from previous chapters, these voices followed Buddy into the darkness of solitary confinement. With no drugs to drown out the noise we know that he attempted to end it all in suicide. In the darkness of this moment he started to clearly hear his other self.

When he came out on the other side of the darkness, Buddy had a relationship with his inner voice. He understood the strength he had within to overcome through the power of faith and belief. The only voice that was left was his. From that point forward, he made a new purpose to learn to trust it and cultivate it into a weapon that would transcend any fear that would try to get in his way.

Buddy realized something profound after his rebirth: God, infinite intelligence, higher power, had given us this world, the natural laws that govern it, our bodies, life, the ability to think and make decisions, and the ability to create the life that we envisioned for ourselves. It would be selfish of us to pray and ask for more. He would show his appreciation through the way he lived, and he would walk in thankfulness and appreciation through action, not words, for the universe already knew his heart.

Peter O'Toole said something kind of funny about this inner relationship with our other-selves or our higher consciousness. He said, "When did I realize I was God? Well, I was praying and suddenly realized I was talking to myself."

Our faith in something higher than ourselves is what makes God a truth for us to believe. The only fact that we have is the power that we have to listen to the direction that comes from within and make decisions that change the direction of our lives. When we speak things in faith and then allow that faith to motivate our action, then we attain those things that we desire. Our tangible belief motivates our actions, which in turn produces results in our lives. Even for those who believe that there is no higher power, it is vital that this person have faith in the direction that he is taking his life, never allowing fear to get in the way of his vision. This person still has to have a relationship with his inner strength because life will test his perseverance. "We are all islands in a common sea." –Anne Morrow Lindbergh

Coming into prison to the Coffield unit, a lot of men tried to get me to join Islam because my father was Muslim when he did time here, but I wanted to be sure that I was going to heaven and so Christianity was more appealing to me. Plus, it was what I grew up around, it felt natural to me.

I told myself that if I was going to take this path, then I was going all the way in. I immersed myself in the church. I joined the church choir and signed up for the faith-based programs. If they called a prayer call, open prayer on the dorm, then I was there to support the needs of those who needed prayer. We had a Bible study that we held three times a week, and on top of that my own personal daily devotions had me smelling like a Christian.

From within the Christian faith I grew tremendously in my understanding of the power of faith and the tactics of fear that the devil uses to control the minds of the lost. What stagnated me was the cookie cutter image of Christianity that you were supposed to look like, walk like, and talk like. Up close I started to see that a lot of the leaders and those who followed were trying to live up to an external expectation instead of allowing true change to evolve from within. I was trying to be a Christian instead of trying to connect with the spirit of God within.

This whole time those who were leading me were telling me that our way was the only way, but I was seeing dudes with different beliefs make transformations that were mind blowing. The different activities I was involved in started to feel shallow and empty, looking for God from external sources such as preachers and elders was limiting, and Christianity started to feel divisive when it came to relating to others who were on their own quest to find God.

Then I read scriptures that gave me the courage to break free from the shackles of religion and break into an internal relationship with the spirit of God within me.

1 John 2:27— "But the anointing which you have received from Him abides in you; but as the same anointing teaches you concerning all things and is true and is not a lie."

A lightbulb went off within. The whole time I had been looking externally for an understanding of God, when within I had a source that would teach and lead me in all areas!

I never looked back, and I have been free of religions titles since and have been growing spiritually by leaps and bounds as my inner voice confirms truths to me.

Arthur Schopenhauer said, "Religion is the masterpiece of the art of animal training, for it trains people as to how they shall think."

'Inner direction' and having faith in your guiding force is powerful. Many great men have called this connection with the higher part of ourselves many things. The pioneering theorist, Abraham Maslow, (1908-1970) called this connection self-actualization. Maslow believes that our needs are motivated through a hierarchy.

First, he believed that we are motivated by food, shelter, and water, our physiological needs. He believed that after we good on grub we then are motivated to focus on feeling safe and secure. If the world feels predictable to us then he says that we feel safe enough to seek out love, recognition, and respect from others with confidence. This pursuit adds to our self-esteem and once we feel loved we then move into trying to reach self-actualization. To describe these type of people and get a better understanding of the characteristics they possess he studied great men and found that they were connected to who they were and understood their purpose in life, they were never stagnated by the opinions of others, and had seemed to have conquered the tendency to conform. He found that they had found their calling and spent most of their time and energy in pursuit of this vision. Overall, he found that they possessed a self-awareness that led them to what he felt, in his opinion, was the last step in our hierarchy of needs- self transcendence!

In this stage of our lives we have transcended the limitations of self and we are operating in line with our destiny. We understand the meaning of life, and we have the power to lead others towards the meaning of life. Like all great leaders, life becomes about freeing others through leading them to their own revelation of inner strength and transcendence of self.

When we are no longer moved and motivated by our basic needs and senses, and we are moved by a deeper essence of who we are beyond the flesh, then we have entered the phase of our lives where not only does the wisdom we carry heal and take our lives to new heights, but we are God like in the way of being able to bring others to their personal internal light the way our higher power brings us to ours. The ability to transform lives and bring light to the world is the essence of what spirituality is.

Living externally through religion is more appealing to some. All one has to do is follow a few traditions, pray a certain number of times a day, and go to church once a week, and you good. Going into self for these people represents going into darkness.

Cyril Connolly said a mouth full when he said, "We are all serving a life sentence in the dungeon of self."

Because most of our souls (mind, will, and emotions) have been scared, battered, and abused; it's best if we don't go deep within to connect with the pain of these wounds. It's best to believe that God will do all the work for you if you just believe he will. Religion tells us to just pray, believe, and wait on God to do the work.

Let me ask you a question, would you raise a kid and then send him into the world without the ability to think, without belief in his ability to problem solve, one who has to call on you every decision, and has not the ability to learn from his pain? Or, would you send a son out into the world who is connected to the wisdom that you have placed within his mind and soul, one who uses that wisdom to make wise choices, and can draw on your words and make adjustments when needed? One who knows that you are there when things get dark but does not use you as a crutch to enable poor choices. When they do call you, it's to thank you for the example and wisdom that you have imparted and not to ask you for money or another handout after you have already given so much. One whom takes the light that you have imparted and gives that light to not only your grandchildren, but to as many people as he can inspire?

When Franz Kafka said "it is often safer to be in chains than to be free," he hinted to the mindsets of people who feel safer in the constraints of religion than to have to manage the responsibility of freedom that comes with being accountable for your own life and having to dig deep in self-reflection for answers to the path that leads to transcendence, and a true relationship with higher intelligence.

Think about the movie *Shawshank Redemption*. The old-school Brooks had a religion called prison life. Brooks had done 50 flat in prison. He had a system that was set by the system that he had grown accustomed to. The system gave him his identity, made him an important man, gave him his sense of purpose. After 50 years the parole board finally granted him his freedom. Brooks went from being 'Brooks the librarian' and having a religion to follow to just being another old man in a fast-moving world. Because he hadn't cultivated his own personal inner voice of purpose and direction, he now was lost out at sea with no way back to shore. It was just too much. One day, in his hotel room, he pulled up a chair, stepped up on it, carved into the banister "Brooks was here," slipped the noose around his neck, and ended it all.

In this chapter, it is our hope to convey the importance of relationship versus religious practices. A wise man once said that, "Going to church does not make you a Christian any more than going to the garage makes you a car." (smile) If anything that we have said can motivate you to connect to your inner spirit for direction and purpose, let it be the fact that "God ain't gone do it for you!" He has given us this world, the laws that govern it, such as sowing and reaping, he has given us intelligence, and the ability to create and think and reproduce...Most of all, he has given us his grace. Let's not be selfish and want more, but to rely on the wisdom that he leads us with from within and let us not be controlled and stagnated by the restraints of religious institutions that confuse and divide us.

We leave you with the wisdom of Buddha, "We are what we think. All that we are arises with our thoughts. With our thought we make our world."

KEYS TO FREEDOM

If the cell represents going into the mind, the Chapel represents going into the soul, or spirit of a man. In order for a person to gain inner peace the spiritual side of themselves must be explored. Life is a series of challenges that stimulates the mind, body, and spirit of a man. It's through these challenges that we find our meaning and become enlightened individuals.

The spiritual realm exists all around us. It exists in the energy of people, places, and even the animals that we share this life with. Modern man has been taught that energy exists outside of himself as a separate part of reality. But, in truth, man is energy and so is thought.

It's not by accident that when we encounter people or places with negative energy or dispositions that we instantly feel drained of our vigor and creativity. These people and places are in a spiritual energy crisis within themselves that they haven't yet conquered. This is the first of many challenges we will face in becoming enlightened.

At each phase of our spiritual growth, we will be tested. It is through these test that we gained wisdom about our purpose and why we were created. In learning to connect to the spiritual side of self, first learn the step in the cell. By learning to control your mind, then, through practice of meditation and self-evaluation, we can connect into the spiritual side of ourselves. Spirituality is man's way of finding God within himself.

YEAR #15: PAROLE

I f nirvana is the final beatitude that transcends suffering, karma, and samsara in Buddhism, and self-transcendence is the highest level of self that one can reach based on the theory of Maslow, then to every prisoner in America, parole has to be the apex. Parole is the Holy Grail of doing time, everything that you do leads to that date, leads to that opportunity to start over and regain infinite possibility. Even for the man who knows that he will die in prison, parole remains a distant fantasy, a daydream, and pieces of this elusive dream are obtained in any way one can get them: a piece of gum, a free world haircut, entering a relationship with a guard, etc. This purpose of freedom lives in the consciousness and sleeps in the unconscious, it is always with you.

TDCJ feels that "parole is a privilege, not a right!" In their eyes, it's a signed contract saying that you agree to doing the remainder of your sentence in the free world under strict supervision.

As with all forms of freedom, there are requirements that need to be met before one can obtain it. TDCJ is no different. Before parole is granted, the parole board, who is responsible for voting must verify that you have served a sufficient amount of time. They must see evidence of transformation that shows that you are no longer a risk to public safety, and that you have a support system in place that will allow you to reside there until you're independent-capable.

Printed in the fine print at the bottom of this contract is a trap for most, the reason why something can look like freedom and not truly be. In the Texas Government Code, 08.181, it requires offenders to return to their legal county of residence after their release. There are loopholes to this rule, but for the most part, men and women have to return to the very places and influences that contributed to the habits and bad choices they made before prison.

This illusion of freedom is seen in the mindset of the men and women who make parole but leave with incarcerated minds. The high recidivism rate in Texas is fed by the mental cages that leaves with men and women who leave physically free but caged and bound by drugs, emotional trauma within the soul that is unresolved, a lack of vision, fear of failure, and indecisiveness. These are the proverbial second time, third time, fourth time losers. They do what it takes to gain the tangible form of freedom but never put in the work to free their minds from the generational curses that have plagued them and their families for centuries.

On the other hand, you have your individuals here right now in prison who will never set foot in the free world again, ever! But when I tell you that they understand the true meaning of freedom you can take that and run with it. These individuals are not looking back at their mistakes and bad choices and choosing to be down on themselves. They take pride in the lessons and the wisdom that have come from their shortcomings. How many of us continue to look back instead of looking forward toward the success and vision of our future? These individuals choose to be happy about the remainder of the life they have left, thankful that they are still alive and not in the grave. With this life that they have and the breath that remains in their lungs they have found a purpose. These men and women can be seen expressing their wisdom and joy through poetry, singing songs at talent shows, writing books that inspire, and laughing with their friends and family on the phone as if they were there with them at a family reunion. These individuals have a strong connection and appreciation for God, their higher power, and they share wisdom with the many young men and women that they cross paths with so that just maybe something that was said may save one from a life sentence in prison.

Ludwig Wittgenstein said something powerful when he said, "A man will be imprisoned in a room with the door that's unlocked and opens inward; as long as it does not occur to them to pull rather than push." Very few people in the world we live in understand that the locked doors of our minds open inwards! Instead of pulling ourselves out from under fear, poverty, brokenness, shame, and hate we continue to push doors closed that the universe tries to open for us to walk through! Inward into the darkness lies the keys to freedom! Only we can unlock the doors that keep us enslaved, no one else has the key!

In society today many people are on parole who have never even been to prison. Every time a parolee goes in to pay his fees or to see his parole officer he is reminded that his freedom can be taken from him with one false move. It's almost like his parole officer is waiting and this realization keep this man cautions at all times. The limitations of parole limit his travel and keep him stuck in certain jobs so that it looks as though he is worthy of the freedom he was given.

See, that is the first mistake, you must first give yourself freedom. Some people in society are on parole because their freedom is borrowed. The fees that they pay is with the energy and time that is drained by fear of failure and hopelessness. Their movement is limited to the limits that the world has told them to adopt within their subconsciousness. They are physically free but limited to where they can go, who they can be around, and fear is always waiting for them to slip up so that it can rob them of their physical freedom (their life).

Again, we remind you of what Mahatma Gandhi said, "The moment the slave resolves that he will no longer be a slave, his fetters fall. He frees himself and shows the way to others. Freedom and slavery are mental states!"

Allow us through *Escaping the Pen* to show you the way. You first have to give yourself freedom! Those who are on parole, who have free minds, make their parole officers feel the power in their vision. They motivate their parole officers to loosen normal restrictions so as not to stop the upward momentum of their greatness and achievement. Their passion is their permission! They don't go into the parole office as a slave asking; their drive and passion speaks in a way that tells their parole officers the next step they are about to take, while at the same damn time, making the parole officer feel like they are a part of the journey and somehow in control! Freedom is in your belief; you have to first give it to yourself by believing in you and fighting for your vision and where you are going. If you wait for someone or something outside of yourself to give you freedom, it will never come, my friend. How do you think great men like Ryan Moody have achieved the greatest form of parole even before stepping foot out into free society? He went inward and connected with the spirit of freedom that had been waiting on him all along.

At the genesis of this book, Moody introduced himself through the forward. We told you that we would get into the power of how his life affected both my boy Buddy and I in some of the same ways at different times and seasons in our journeys. It's amazing because at the time of the writing of this amazing book that's about to shake the world (smile), Moody is actually my co-worker in the ODR. He is actually the reason that I got hired, he put his name behind my character.

I came to Coffield in late 2011/early 2012, new to the journey of change. I knew that I attained something different, but I hadn't really ever seen an example of what different was. The first few years here of trying to find my path, I would hear stories of my father and the way he did his time on the Coffield unit. My pops was a big dude, muscular, and was a part of the weightlifting team. One name that kept coming up during these stories was 'Big Moody.' He had been on the weightlifting team back in the day and it was rumored that he knew my dad very well.

My dad had left my life as a young kid and anyone who knew my dad very well and could fill in gaps as to the personality and history of my father, I wanted to talk to.

I put the word out that I was looking for him, "Tell him Bobby J. Haddock son need to speak with him." I don't remember exactly where we were when we had our first conversation or exactly what was said, but the strength in his demeanor was readily apparent. He wasn't massively big; I could clearly see why most people put the big in front of his last name though.

Years later, while on my personal spiritual journey, I got the privilege of being on the same faith-based dorm with him. It was here that we really connected and got to know one another. He filled me in greatly about my pops, conversations that I will never forget and are the ones that allowed me to finally see what different was.

I'll never forget the time I was standing at his cubical on the faith-based dorm just talking about life when he said, "Bro, I'm gone tell you the truth. If I don't ever go home, I'm already free in Christ. I'm going to wake up daily with joy and touch as my people for the kingdom as I can. I'm at home in my heart."

It was at this moment that I truly understood the difference between religion and relationship. In his soul, through his eyes, I could see freedom, purpose, peace, and inner strength. His light was going to motivate you to do one thing or the other. Either you avoided crossing his path so as to avoid feeling your dark spots exposed by his light, or you dressed yourself in his motivation and allowed it to dig deep within to your next level, your other self, the Spirit of God within you.

What is most amazing about being around Moody is seeing this consistency in his walk. Purpose guides his days, and he walks in the knowledge of knowing that grace covers his step and favor goes before him.

Having the privilege of working side by side with him over these past two years has given me a deeper look into his mind than most get to see. What's amazing is that he has struggles, just like the rest of us! The exclamation point is for the fact that form the outside you wouldn't be able to tell. Another thing one wouldn't be able to tell is that for over fifteen years he was in the game, hustling in prison, making moves. Today, he is grounded in his vision and purpose and he walks in that light with consistency daily, his foundation never wavering. "We are what we repeatedly do, excellence then is not an act, but what we do." –Unknown

My lil-Bro, Buddy, met Moody early 2019. Buddy has been driven by and motivated by competition for most of his life. Since he discovered working out and bodybuilding, he has strived to be the best and Moody's name kept popping up in workout circles as being the best. Buddy couldn't wait to get his chance to size Moody up.

He finally got his chance to meet up with the ever-elusive Moody when they moved him to the dorms. The dorm 2C was out at P6 and it was one of the bigger dorms.

One day Buddy was talking to this dude named Lucas about his passion for working out and bodybuilding when Lucus said that he wanted to introduce him to someone who was passionate about the physical grind. Lucas made the introductions and when he said the name 'Moody,' Buddy's ear perked up. Tall, with an athletic build, solid and in shape to be in his forties, Buddy shook his hand feeling like the legend was bigger than the man.

They chopped it up some more about different routines and ways to build muscle and by the end of the conversation they agreed to be workout partners.

Buddy couldn't wait to show him who the man was. With him being 28 there was no way he was going to let an old school out do him on the workout. That first week of working out with Moody went smooth. Intense, but nothing to say the man was a legend. What Buddy didn't know was that he had fell into Moody's trap, countless workout partners of Moody's had survived the first week to only tap out after he turned up the heat.

That second week while changing into his workout clothes, Buddy got his first glimpse of Moody with his shirt off. Separation and definition were on point, now things were starting to make sense. That week Buddy was tested physically and mentally in ways that he had never been tested.

The strength of his heart and his pride wouldn't allow him to tap out like the rest. Moody shook his hand and gave him his card, validated his willpower.

There is nothing like seeing another level in someone whom you admire to get you going. Working out with Moody not only showed Buddy why Moody was a legend on Coffield, it showed him that he had a lot of areas that he could reach higher in. In conversations about life with Moody he was inspired to continue to reach higher in his thoughts, and even in spiritual life he started a journey to deeper understanding his own personal beliefs.

Most amazing was the day that Buddy found out that Moody had a 99-year sentence and had been locked up over 20 plus years! Where did this man get his hope, his fire, his determination, his smile, his peace? When he asked Moody, Moody said, " Romans 5:3-4 says, 'that we glory in tribulation, knowing that tribulation produces perseverance, and perseverance character, and character, hope.' Bro, just as a physical exercise produces muscle, I have used the tribulations of my life to build up the strength of my character and now I carry around a hope that comes from true freedom of knowing that God's grace walks within me through all that we brace."

Buddy left that conversation having witnessed true freedom and understanding that there are no shortcuts to true greatness. He would use the journey of life and its lessons to find true freedom, that is the key.

It's amazing that the very scripture that Moody gave to Buddy as his reason for freedom is the very premise of our entire book! We have discussed in each and every chapter how darkness and tribulation can be used to find the light within. Wow just think how much growth would take place if everyone understood the freedom equation of (pain plus character equals hope and freedom). Scott Peck said as much when he said, "As Benjamin Franklin said, those things that hurt, instruct. It is for this reason that wise people learn not to dread but actually to welcome problems and actually to welcome the pain of problems." Just as those of us who make parole and reenter the free world have stipulations that limit how and when we move (for the most part), those who are free physically in society but bound in their thinking put stipulations on how far they can climb as well.

Those who make parole with bound minds reenter society focused on gratification, trying to make up for lost time, and just living for the day. They are bound by the desires of the flesh, the limitations of their minds, and a drifters mentality. They remain in mental prisons which won't take long to manifest itself into physical reality.

Those who make parole with free minds tend to get out with a vision! Our focus is on our opportunity at redemption, we have a strong desire to reconnect with family ties that were loosened while we were incarcerated, our focus is on retribution.

If you get nothing from this book, we at the bare minimum need you to understand that the parole of life is obtained through the freedom of your mind and spirit. In order to reach this destination, there are requirements one must go through: one must soul search and go inward, into the dark places and face those fears, traumas, and mental cycles head on. You must break free and grab hold the keys that will unlock the chains that have you bound from reaching your true potential and destiny. These chains can present themselves in laziness which paralyzes forward movement and causes one to procrastinate and put things off till next time. The chains can show up as a competency which caused us to settle for just believing something instead of reaching for our true desires and dreams. One of the main ways that these chains show up is in the form of generational patterns and behaviors. Ways of living, thinking, and operating that get passed down and the consequences of these behaviors follow as well. I experienced this firsthand, my father did 13 years on this same exact unit and when it's all said and done, I will have done 15 years in prison with 10 on this unit. It's not a game. The chains of our minds must be broken and for this to happen we must have the courage to free ourselves.

Thomas H. Huxley said it best when he said, "It is far better for a man to go wrong in freedom than to go right in chains!"

Buddy and I have made up our minds that we would rather die on the road of freedom than to feel safe in mental chains. Harriet Tubman who is famously known for the underground railroads that freed thousands of slaves felt the same way that we do, you free yourself, then you fight to free others from the darkness of their cages and this is the exactly what she did for those she could. The sad reality is that not everyone wants to be freed, they have become comfortable in their chains and what is even a greater atrocity is the fact that that many who are bound don't even know it.

"I freed a thousand slaves. I could have freed a thousand more if only they knew they were slaves." –Harriet Tubman.

Sometimes I close my eyes and imagine what it would feel like to dig deep within myself and muster up the courage to go on this journey with my life on the line or at the very least more pain and suffering, but I determined that my freedom is worth it. I take off on this journey not really knowing the exact road that I should take, but I know that I'm going to no go north with determination in my soul and the help of loyal friends and family along the way, I take it one day at a time allowing God's grace to go before me each day that I wake up and take the road to freedom once more. I imagine that someone that I have been traveling with finally says that we have "made it north," or "we are free," we belong to no one but ourselves and God and that we can build a life of respect. I imagine the feeling of truly being free and knowing that it all started with the courage and one step of north. I often wondered why people say, "down south" and "up north;" when I think about the work that has to be done to pull yourself up from the darkness, I no longer have to wonder.

And really when I think about it, I no longer have to worry what that slave felt like because me and my lil-bro Buddy have been both been the slaves within ourselves. We know what it's like to have to muster up the courage to pull ourselves from the darkness of our minds and take that first step toward freedom within. We know what its like to wake up, day in and day out, and face the challenges of the daily grind to get 'north' and finally hear the voice within tell us that we have finally made it and that we can now manifest the life that we dream of.

Both Buddy and I have come a long way on this road to freedom; we have attained the most powerful form of freedom in our souls, and yet still await our chance at the physical reality of another chance on the other side of these gates.

It is our trust and hope, that the day will come when we cross paths with you and we are blessed to hear that one thing that we have shared from our stories have helped to liberate one of you from the chains that at one time or another enslaved us all.

Freedom will only come to those who are determined to go after it with a relentless spirit. It must be a chief aim, a definite goal and purpose or we end up in a state that Robert Heinlein described when he said, "In the absence of clearly defined goals, we become strangely loyal to performing daily trivia until ultimately we become enslaved by it."

"Free yourselves!"

KEYS TO FREEDOM

If I were to ask you, like Morpheus asked Neo in the movie *The Matrix*, to take either the red pill or the blue pill and gave you a description of both pills. One being the blue pill--you stay asleep and continue your life as nothing ever happened, with everything around you staying the same. But, while alone you know deep down in your soul that there is more to life, that your doubt, your beliefs, your limitations were all at some point overcomable. Would you still take the blue pill?

Let's just imagine that you've decided that there's more to life than being stuck in a dead-end job, bad relationship, or negative environment that robs you of your time and energy; that there is more to life and that you could have the life of your dreams; that you could be free in mind, body, and spirit rather than a slave to circumstances, even more that the only limits in life are the ones we place on ourselves. Would you take the red pill?

Escaping the pen is our red pill to you. We've done the hard time, so that you, the reader, never have to personally experience prison. But physical time can't compare to the mental time we do in our poor thinking and the time we waste in bad situations and relationships.

Understand, freedom starts in our thinking way before we see parole. By becoming free in our minds, hearts, and spirit, we can become teachers and leaders. Teaching others that the only limitations in life are the ones we place on ourselves. I believe this is a step towards achieving that goal. This is the ultimate key to freedom.

CONCLUSION:

————◦❦◦————

I t is amazing that when we first started this journey of writing *Escaping the Pen*, we didn't know how much we would grow through writing the principles of our souls on paper. One of the most amazing things that served as confirmation that this book was destined to be written was how, when we were finished outlining each year concept, the number of years were exactly fifteen!

When we thought about it, we realized that fifteen was significant because in Buddy's case, he had exactly a fifteen year sentence, and as for me, I have to do exactly fifteen years before I am eligible to be released back into society. For us this book is a manifestation in the exact manner that mirrors the lessons and beliefs that act as fuel within our souls on a daily basis. Yoko Ono said, "I saw sorrow turning into clarity." We understand exactly what she felt when she said those words. The sorrow that we felt while in the darkness of this prison have given us clarity in what it takes to "escape the pen" in all areas that we face in this life.

"But fifteen years," a lot of you would exclaim, "that's a lot of wasted time." First, we agree and for that exact reason it is vital that you apply the principles from this book to the relevant areas of your life. Second, when it comes to time, we look at it like Frederick Nietzsche when he said, "In the dark time feels different than when it is light."

When you are stressed, and the day has been long, and you just need to get away and slow things, what do you do? You close your eyes! When you close your eyes and darkness engulfs your consciousness, everything slows down, and you are able to see inside of your head and heart in a more precise manner. It's in this manner that we have used the darkness of prison; To slow down and find freedom within.

We hope that the fifteen-year journey was as fun and fulfilling for you as it was for us. From the intake system all the way to the freedom of parole, there has been a calculated, step-by-step flow of lessons that build upon one another. If you missed the lessons that you are supposed to learn from the intake process in prison, you will definitely be lost in the sauce when you get to work call, cases, and grievances.

It is the same way with the education system; you have to learn basic math such as addition and subtraction before you are able to handle algebra and complex concepts that need to be known for calculus. In our personal lives, if we fail to carry the lessons that we gained from life, trials, and tribulations with us as we grow, then we inevitably set ourselves up for failure in the future.

We just seen a dynamic example of this truth yesterday. This dude, whose name is Gypsy, had got through the rules of the intake system, he had made it through the celly stage and had earned his way to the dorms, but he was stuck in dayroom. He was still influenced by his environment and the examples that it's set for behavior. Yesterday, a female officer came into the dorm and instructed us to not change the TV from the safety channel. Gypsy had been drinking and so he got into a silly confrontation with this woman and ended up walking up to the TV in pride and changing the channel, basically bucking, or disobeying the female guard (pride). Well, long story short, he was handcuffed and escorted to seg. This is the kicker, the entire time he was putting up a fuss over the television he had a cell phone on him. When they got him to seg and stripped him out, they found it!

Vincent Van Gogh said, "If one is a master of one thing and understands one thing well, one has at the same time insight into and understating of many things." In the intake year we talked about understanding the it's not where you start but where you finish. If Gypsy would have established his finish in the beginning, the influences of dorm life couldn't have motivated his actions. It is our hope that as you go through the remainder of your life, you allow the lessons that you encounter to build upon one another and guide you.

If you would have asked either me or Buddy what vision, freedom, faith, direction, or purpose was fifteen years ago, we wouldn't have had the answer because the darkness hadn't revealed the answers yet. George Eliot said, "The important work of moving the world forward does not wait to be done by perfect men." Through our pain, and in our still current imperfection, it is our prayer that you escape the pens of your life and enter a freedom that can serve to set someone else free.

The End.

If you would like to contact the authors, feel free to reach out at:

Bobby Bowen
1619547
or
Donderick Walker
1893182

Coffield Unit
2661 FM 2054
Tennessee Colony, TX 75884

Glossary

Big Homie- a name commonly given to an individual who has muscle and carries himself with respect.

Celly- the person who a man or woman in prison shares a cell with.

Cell Time- the time that two individuals who share a cell split in order to get personal time themselves.

Cell Block- the housing area in prison where cells are located.

Chowtime- a word that signifies that it's time to go eat breakfast, lunch, or dinner.

Cluck out- the act of getting in trouble in a dumb or foolish way that could have been avoided.

C.O.- corrections officer; a common abbreviated name for a guard.

Covesha- Nickname for COVID-19

Doing Time- mentally, spiritually, physically being engaged in your sentence, consciously focused on growth.

Free World- anything outside prison gates and free society.

Getting it Out the Mud- Used to describe anything one obtains from the struggle.

Good- a term that is used to describe a male or female officer who is not strict or by-the-book.

Good Money- any item on commissary that can be consumed, i.e. chips, coffee, or soda. Also used to describe payment for something that is said or done that is stupid, i.e. punch in the arm or face on the wall.

Green- a term used to describe a person who is naïve about prison life.

Heart- used to describe a person who has courage.

Hooch- penitentiary moonshine.

Inmate.com- information that is passed mouth to mouth in prison.

In the Game- describes a person who uses contraband to make money.

In Ya Feelings- a term used to describe a person who is emotional.

In the World- to daydream about free society.

Jack Game- A group of people who masturbate on female guards.

Kites- a small handwritten letter that is passed hand to hand in prison.

Lacing Up- to inform a person on a particular aspect of prison life that he didn't know.

Lion Mindset- self-belief, vision, purpose, and determination; in one's thinking while doing time.

Messin' Wit Them Boyz- a term that describes a person in prison who engages in homosexual activity.

Overstood- emphasis on the word 'understood.'

Off the Streets- anything bought with commissary from another individual on the dorms or in the hallways.

Peek Mirror- a small handheld mirror used to look outside a cell and down the runway.

Penitentiary Games- a term used to describe any type of con to meet one's objective.

Passing Time- passively going through the motions during a prison sentence, i.e., excessively playing board games and watching TV.

Policing- a term used to describe an officer who goes overboard in enforcing the rules.

Rack Up- a term officers use to clear the dayroom and put people back in their cell.

Slaving- a term used to describe a person who feels he has no other choice to work in prison.

Size Up- making a mental assessment on the threat level of another individual.

Spread- food off of commissary that is prepared in a creative way.

Store- a term used to describe going to commissary.

Stamps- postage stamps bought off of commissary used to buy extra food.

T-Jones- a term used to mean 'mother.'

Walk of Shame- when an individual's commissary card is given back to them with no money and they can't buy food.

ABOUT THE AUTHORS

Bobby "King B" Bowen's father shot his mother when he was only 7. With his father in prison and his mother fighting to survive in more ways than one way, he was lead into the streets for direction. Gang life in Wichita Falls, TX lead to TYC (Texas Youth Commission) and after a short time of freedom, he received a 30 year sentence in prison. This is where his King was born. Through soul searching, education, and a commitment to growth, he lives a King's mentality daily as he awaits his physical freedom. His favorite quote is, "The facts of our lives are not as important as our attitude towards them."

Donderick "Buddy" Walker started learning hard life lessons early on. Growing up in tough neighborhoods, he learned early on to fight for the things he wanted in life. After being relocated in San Antonio, TX at 15 from Jefferson Parish, LA due to hurricane Katrina, he got a fresh start in a new city. But like most things, this lead to more growing pains. At 22 years old, he got sentenced to do 15 years in prison; this is where he finally became a man and found his purpose in life was to become an entrepreneur, author, and personal trainer. His favorite quote is, "Be good to the game and the game will be good to you".

CPSIA information can be obtained
at www.ICGtesting.com
Printed in the USA
BVHW091149050122
625458BV00011B/397